Legendary Northwoods Animals

Legendary Northwoods Animals

By Galen Winter

Illustrations by John Boettcher

WILLOW CREEK PRESS

Minocqua, Wisconsin

ISBN# 1-57223-009-6

Published by Willow Creek Press
         Outlook Publishing
         PO Box 881
         Minocqua, WI 54548
         1-800-850-WILD

Library of Congress Cataloging-in-Publication Data

Winter, Galen.
     Legendary northwoods animals / by Galen Winter : illustrations by
John Boettcher.
       p.   cm.
     ISBN 1-57223-009-6
     1. Animals, Mythical—Northwestern States. 2. Animals, Mythical—
Northeastern States.   I. Boettcher, John. II. Title.
GR825.W497   1994
398.24'5'0974--dc20   94-29223
                                                          CIP

Printed in the U.S.A.

FOREWORD

By Professor Norbert Hefflefinger, Ph.D.

I'm real sorry I let Winter get my stuff on funny animals you can find up north. I never shoulda oughta signed that contract. He's gonna make a lotta money an' I'm gittin' peanuts.

PREFACE

Humor can be gentle. Sarcasm is harsh. Falling between those extremes are irony and satire. All can be entertaining, enhancing both nonsense and knowledge. But whatever the form of expression, wit is required to effectively tell a tall tale.

Readers count on a Galen Winter column to be funny and stylish, as is this book, *Legendary Northwoods Animals*. It requires a special kind of wit to dream up and then diddle with myth in an effort to create future folklore in contemporary prose.

Winter wit originates way out in right field; then roams the entire outfield, picking off everything from pop-ups behind second base to long balls off the center-field wall.

Although he pulls up short of sarcasm, readers don't have to excavate for nuggets of irony and satire which lend sparkle to the gems of humor. Sparing no one and finding nothing sacred, nonetheless Winter doesn't bludgeon nor crucify.

So, writing a good introduction is impossible. Attempts at levity fall short of the master's strokes, doing a "straight" who–what–when–where report doesn't do a quirky work justice. In this book of nonsense, a thread of snobbishness prevents each tale from degenerating into a wallow of slapstick. Winter obviously isn't writing for TV viewers when he pulls legendary "rabbits" out of his hat. *Legendary Northwoods Animals*, by design, is for *readers*, not skimmers and viewers. As a retired attorney and still active sportsman, Winter must have delighted in sucking in witnesses and waterfowl over the decoys before delivering the *coup de grace*.

Being (figuratively) shot down becomes fun when preceded by feeding calls that sound like the real thing and glimpses of golden corn used to illegally bait the shallows in front of the blind. The mix of outrageous imagination and snide commentary on the foibles of folks who take themselves too seriously is a rare blend.

But I do have a suggestion. Nibble on this book. If read in one sitting, it loses its potency. Read a chapter each evening as you would a magazine column. Winter is accustomed to writing humorous vignettes for the "back page" of sporting magazines. While hardly as well known as some pioneers in that genre (like Ed Zern of *Field & Stream)*, the antics and writings of Galen Winter are legendary in Shawano County...a thinly populated Wisconsin jurisdiction containing the Stockbridge-Munsee (Mohican) Indian reservation, bordered by the Menominee reservation on the north and just a few miles west of the Oneida tribal lands in Brown County.

As a satirical social commentary, Winter's description of the Ognib and the Onisac (two celebrated protective spirits concerned with the welfare of northern Native American tribes) is hard to top. But he chips in with other imaginative legends such as the Diaphanous Moose, the Woose Grock, the Woodtick Hawk, the Antlered Brown Trout, the Lumberjack Parrot and a myriad of other backwoods denizens.

Even the wildest of imaginations (if you question whether Winter is a crack shot or a deft dry fly caster, just ask *him* and you'll get answers as exaggerated as the tales in this book) requires stimulation. Should the man ever deign to grace your kitchen for longer than 10 minutes, that which sustains the natural wit and kick-starts the fantasies will become readily apparent. He can seriously erode a well-stocked liquor cabinet and doesn't blanch at puffing "outside" cigars.

As behooves a lawyer, sportsman and literary gentleman, there's usually something left in a bottle after he leaves; largely because his taste in booze is so catholic once the single-malt Scotch is gone, he finds it impossible to decide whether to finish out the sour-mash Bourbon, Straight Rye or Imported Vodka.

His most noteworthy shortcomings as a human being, however, are making promises he has no intention of keeping, and a total lack of map-reading ability, which makes the grouse and deer-hunting forays and trout-fishing adventures he brags about suspect.

As an apology for taking a fellow scribe's name in vain (via a misspelling) when advising "go soak your head" in a Winter treatise on gun-dog training entitled, "To Hell with Dave Duffey," the Shawano barrister–author promised to bring along a jug of my favorite sourmash, Maker's Mark, the next time he was clipping off rural mailboxes while touring the Tilleda area. But he vowed he didn't know where to obtain such esoteric mash to go with the splash from the Embarrass River's north branch.

Suspecting a nonperformance ploy, I drew a detailed map to guide Winter from his office in Shawano to the liquor store on Main Street in Marion, just over the Waupaca County line.

He showed up the other day, sans jar of whisky, with a typically shameless and ingenious proposal. If I'd write the foreword to *Legendary Northwoods Animals*, he'd bribe me with *two* jugs of Maker's Mark. That cost would appear in an expense account he'd forward the the book's publisher, Tom Petrie. "In the event Tom falls for it, I'll send one to you."

As you read this, know that there is time for many a sip between the writing and the publishing of a book. The appearance of these words in print is proof that I've discharged a duty to an imaginative fellow bird hunter who asked for a favor. But don't bet that any sippin' whisky that's gone down my hatch between the birth and conception of this introduction has been paid for by anyone but yours truly.

—David Michael Duffey

Contents

INTRODUCTION

When I was a mere lad, my father returned from a fishing trip—four days late. Since grandmother visited us during that time, and had returned to her home only the day before father reappeared, I knew there was a very good reason why he was late.

Certainly he wouldn't want to miss an opportunity to talk with his mother-in-law. She brought me candy. Mother was quite interested in why he was late. I have a vague recollection of some shouting and a broken vase.

Mother apparently did not believe father's explanation, but seemed perfectly reasonable to me. I had learned, only a few weeks before in Sunday School, of another occurrence where a man was swallowed by a large fish.

I came to father's defense, telling mother she was indeed lucky to have father back so soon, recalling to her attention that Jonah had to spend a substantially longer time in the stomach of the large fish that had swallowed him.

Father rewarded me for my loyalty by taking me along the next evening when the pre-dusk hatch of Brown Drakes put the trout into a feeding frenzy. And thus began my lifelong interest in the rare and odd creatures which even now inhabit the northern forests.

As you carefully study this text, the scholar will note the absence of some of the more common legendary northwoods animals. The Hodag and the Minocki come to mind. If you are disappointed by the exclusion of those animals, well, that's just too bad. I'm the one who wrote this book, not you. And I'm sick and tired of constant criticism.

Originally, a study of the The Man-Eating Plant was to be included within the text. As a matter of fact, a considerable amount of time and money were spent in finding one and transplanting it into the laboratory. The plan, however, was abandoned when the plant ate my assistant. The laboratory was also abandoned.

In order to be fair about it we also eliminated the study of a counterbalancing but equally strange and peculiar creature, the *Homo vegetarianus*, also known as The Plant-Eating Man.

As my education expanded, I encountered many a rare and exceptional beast. The Roc, the Mermaid, the Unicorn, the Phoenix (as well as the Tucson), the Sphinx, the Gryphon, the Cyclops, and the Dragon all come to mind.

But they all resided in the Old World. What about our hemisphere? Yes, now that it has been brought to your attention, what about the western hemisphere, you may well ask?

With the exception of the Democrat, which has been the subject of ongoing investigation, the study of the bizarre and peculiar creatures of the North American continent have been largely disregarded by the scientific community.

A few tracts have been published by Professor Norbert Hefflefinger. I am indebted to him for his generosity in allowing me to refer to those studies. (And he is indebted to me for my generosity in allowing him the share of my royalties which he demanded.)

And I must, of course, acknowledge and thank those few old lumberjacks still living in VA hospital alcoholic wards who provided accounts of personal adventures involving some of the animals described in this textbook. Unfortunately, my notes are fragmentary and I can't remember their names. I think they were Finnish. Well, you know who you are, so "Thanks."

I can personally attest to the accuracy of all other data appearing in this text. Moreover, while securing that data, in each instance, I had the foresight of taking an unimpeachable witness with me. It's too bad he got eaten by that damned plant.

Galen Winter
August 29, 1994
Shawano, Wisconsin

Part I

Authenticated Legendary Animals

THE DIAPHANOUS MOOSE

(Alces alces invisibilis)

The modern moose species of the Cervidae family can trace its North American roots back to the Pleistocene epoch. (And you thought having an ancestor who came over on the Mayflower was a big deal.)

In colonial times, the range of the moose extended from the Arctic to those portions of the northern forests where the colder temperatures necessary for their health and well-being commonly occurred.

Over the years, however, the elimination and decline of the forest and woodland habitat of the moose have greatly reduced the range of the magnificent animal.

With the exception of Minnesota and Maine and those few other parts of the country which are largely untouched by civilization, the presence of a moose is a rarity. This is understandable. After all, who would want to live in Boston, New York, Detroit or Chicago, or even in the suburbs?

One subspecies, however, has been able to co-exist in developed areas in spite of the transformation of the primeval forests into agricultural land. That subspecies is the *Alces alces invisibilis*—sometimes called the Diaphanous or Invisible Moose.

Endowed with a cellular structure so fine as to make it completely transparent, the Diaphanous Moose has been able to avoid the depredations caused by hunter and predator. Its numbers have remained stable and, according to some naturalists, may have increased.

The ability of the Diaphanous Moose to survive in the wild has been reinforced by the peculiar spoor left by the animal. The print made by one of its feet is the easily recognized five to seven-inch hoof mark common to the other moose subspecies.

JOHN BOETTCHER

But the other three tracks are different. One is quite similar to that of the timber wolf, one is indistinguishable from the track of a cougar, and the third appears to be the footprint of a woodsman's boot.

Tracking the Diaphanous Moose is an impossible task. Wolves and cougars, seeing the track of a human being, think it must be a hunter with a gun and immediately abandon the project and seek out bunny rabbits.

Many human hunters, finding the track of a man following the same animal, presume another hunter is ahead of them and discontinue their hunt. The other hunters doggedly follow the animal for days and never see it.

The successful ability of the animal to escape detection and capture is proven by the fact that no sightings have ever been reported.*

Hunters and ecologists have banded together in an association dedicated to preserving and maintaining the subspecies. Their organization, Invisible Moose Unlimited, holds annual fund-raising banquets and cooperates with landowners and Natural Resource Departments in the development of Invisible Moose preserves.

The Invisible Moose Unlimited group has amassed a considerable treasury earmarked for habitat improvement. During last winter's prolonged sub-zero temperatures, organization volunteers selflessly gave of their time and energy to distribute large quantities of invisible hay to the areas frequented by the animal.

Through their efforts the herds have grown to such an extent some states have allowed selective hunting. Artists are engaged in competitions for the design of Invisible Moose hunt stamps, and invisible moose hunting tags are available to those hunters who are successful in the state sponsored lotteries.**

* The record shows only one specimen has ever been captured. It was sold to the Chicago Brookfield Zoo where it was identified as "Invisible Moose" and displayed to the public. Apparently it was unable to live in captivity and soon died. The exact date of death is unknown. It took the zoo keeper over six months to determine it was no longer alive.

** But one must be careful not to lose the invisible moose tag.

Range of *Alces alces invisibilis*

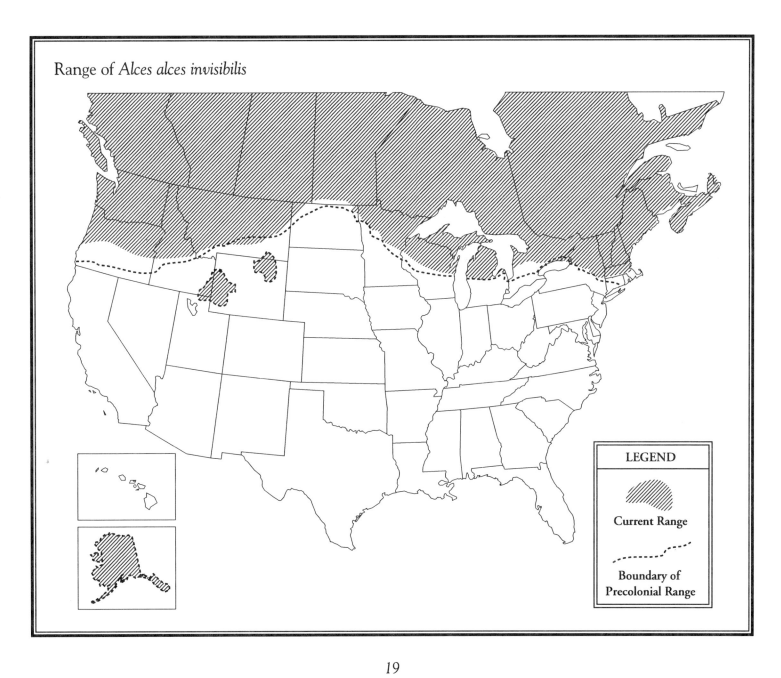

LEGEND

Current Range

Boundary of
Precolonial Range

THE FREDDYCAT

(Felinus geographica septapodicus)

The Bobcat and the Tomcat are well known to the general population of this Republic. Recent studies show almost fifty percent of high school graduates can either identify pictures of them or spell their names.

The Freddycat, however, does not enjoy such widespread recognition. Its obscurity can probably be assigned to the quality of the first scientific study commissioned under a grant from the Department of the Interior.

Professor Norbert Hefflefinger undertook the job and wrote an extensive and learned treatise. Due to a typing mistake in the grant itself, or through the failure of the Professor to carefully read it, a terrible error occurred.

Rather than a study of the Freddycat, the professor investigated the 'Fraidy Cat'. His monograph was extensively published before the error was discovered. Neither the criticism nor the commentaries elicited by the publication captured the scientific community's interest in the Freddycat, and no additional studies were undertaken.

Since the Professor could not find the original grant award document and the Department of Interior had apparently misfiled each of the 500 copies it had made, no one has been able to assign blame for the debacle. Suffice it to say the first serious study of the Freddycat appears herein.

The Freddycat is a tiny and timid migratory animal closely resembling the bobcat. It is commonly found throughout the northern pine forest lowlands during the entire year. Studies show the animal seldom travels more than ten miles from the place of its birth.

This, of course, makes it unique. Nowhere else in the mammalian world is there a record of a migratory

creature which remains year-round in the same locale. Various theories have been suggested to explain this phenomenon.

Some naturalists claim the Freddycat has a very poor sense of direction. They believe it starts out for Florida or Texas but gets lost and always ends up at the same place it starts.

Others theorize the beast's migratory instincts are balanced by a strong feeling of homesickness which increases geometrically as the arithmetic distance between the Freddycat and its natal lair increases. These counterbalancing instincts keep the animal close to its place of birth.

More recently, other explanations have been advanced. One school believes the Freddycat is not truly migratory.

They point out the Freddycat lives in tamarack swamps under the most miserable of conditions— mosquitoes in the summer, constantly up to their knees in water or ice, and all that.

They suggest the Freddycat moves about not because of any migratory instinct but simply because it wants to get out of the swamp. They further claim the animal is unsuccessful in its attempts to escape because it has an uneven number of legs.

Due to some genetic mistake back in the Pliocene epoch, the subspecies known as the Right-Handed Freddycat is missing the left front foreleg. The Left-Handed Freddycat subspecies is missing the right.

When this animal embarks on its frequent journeys to get out of the swamp and onto some high ground, it shares, with all other seven-legged creatures, the characteristic of being unable to travel in a straight line. So, it constantly runs in wide circles—but never with a diameter of more than ten miles—and is doomed to live in the bogs and quagmires forever.

In desperation, some of the Freddycats have written to zoos offering to surrender, provided only that the zoo people would have to come to the swamps and pick them up.

To date, zoo officials, presuming they were dealing with 'Fraidy Cats' who couldn't spell, have accepted none of the offers.

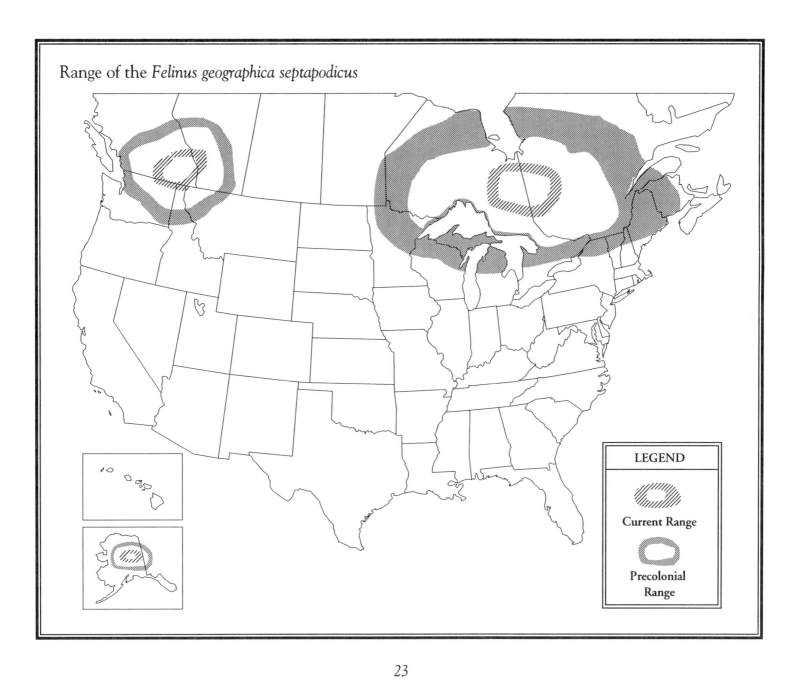

Range of the *Felinus geographica septapodicus*

LEGEND

Current Range

Precolonial
Range

THE ROCKWORM

(Oligochaetus igneous)

The range of the Soft-Shelled Canadian Rockworm extends from the Laurentian Plateau in Labrador in a southerly and westerly direction over the area roughly covered by the glaciers of the Carboniferous and Permian periods of the Paleozoic Era.

Like the Cockroach and the Horseshoe Crab, the Rockworm has survived and looks and acts much like its prehistoric ancestors. This is particularly surprising since the worm is not aggressive and is endowed with few protective defenses.

Certain marine creatures with no hard exoskeletal coverings seek shelter within the abandoned shells of other sea creatures. In a similar manner, the Rockworm protects itself from its enemies by burrowing into rocks and there establishing its residence.

So, too, the Rockworm carries its home with it as it cautiously moves about in search of the silicone on which it exclusively feeds. The Rockworm prefers igneous and metamorphic rocks and is seldom found in lime or sandstone.

Adopting the same color, density and unit weight as the rock it inhabits, the Rockworm is almost impossible to detect. It is shy, timid and, actually, a terrible coward.

Professor Hefflefinger claims that as the Rockworm grows bigger and bigger and inhabits larger and larger rocks, it eventually overcomes its shyness and becomes a boulder creature.

The Rockworm emits no sound whatsoever whenever it is in the presence of other forms of life. When it believes itself threatened, it emulates the opossum, lies perfectly still and looks for all the world just like a dead rock.

The Rockworm will abandon its stone home only

John Boettcher

when it outgrows it and is forced to drill into a larger rock. As it grows and develops, the Rockworm sheds its old home and enters a newer, larger one. The older the worm, the bigger his home.

Geologists long presumed the granite blocks found in the Upper Midwest were dropped by retreating glaciers. They now admit the stones were probably brought there by migrating Rockworms, and the various gravel deposits represent the residue created by the worms chewing into larger rocks as they outgrew their smaller safe havens.

No one knows much about the life cycle of the Rockworm, but from the size of some of the rocks laying around in the north country, they must get to be pretty old.

Many large, well-preserved specimens of the Rockworm have been found. I have a very large one in the lawn of my lakeside cottage. I offered it—free of charge—to the Smithsonian. All they had to do was come and pick it up. They didn't even answer my letter. And they call themselves a museum.

Early settlers were well aware of the existence of the Rockworm. During periods of famine, rocks would be collected and boiled for soup. Unfortunately, the Rockworm has very little protein value, so the settlers starved to death anyway, but it gave them something to do.

Stone soup, made according to the Native American recipe was, we are told, quite savory. The early settlers did not know stone soup became nourishing (and actually delicious) only when the Indian Am fruit had been added to the boiling water.

The American Indians often collected the necessary Ams from the shrubbery on which they grew and which was quite common in colonial days. The plant long ago became extinct.

(But I have clear recollections of my grandfather telling me about the Indian Am bushes.)

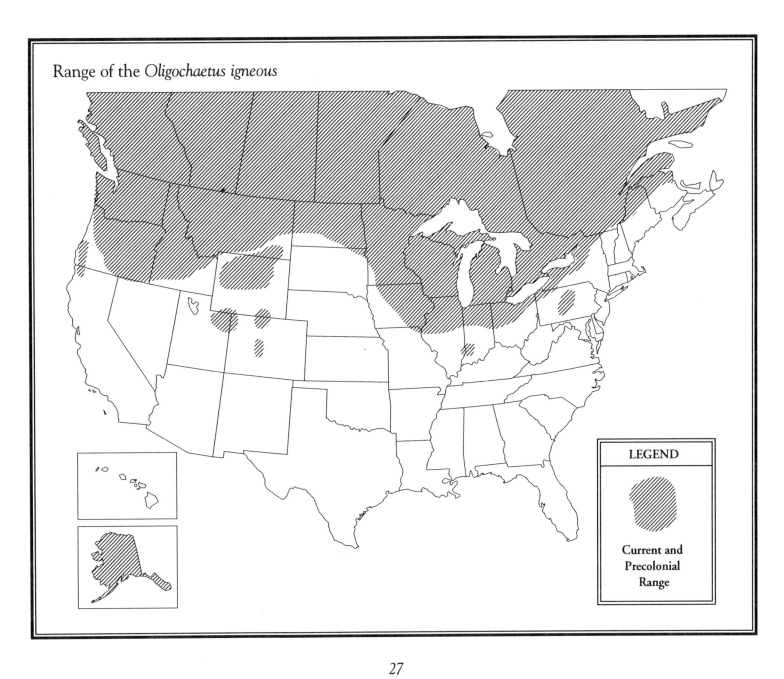

Range of the *Oligochaetus igneous*

LEGEND

Current and
Precolonial
Range

THE NOSEEUMUSKIE

(Esox disappearicus)

In an effort to increase the fisherman tourist trade in the early 1930's, various state Conservation Commissions authorized their Fish Management Divisions to construct hatcheries and experiment with raising and transplanting the fry and fingerlings of the Muskellunge.

One such experiment was a real puzzlement to fish biologists (as well as to human biologists who specialized in fish studies). The Commission removed all fish from a northern lake and planted it with their homegrown Muskie fingerlings. To the surprise of all, the fish never grew larger than 12 inches in length.

In their natural state, the Muskellunge attains lengths in excess of four feet. What kept them from so developing in the experimental lake? Perhaps it was predation.

Hundreds of miles of mosquito netting were stretched over the lake to keep eagle and osprey from attacking the fish. The raptors were successfully kept from the lake, but there still were no fish over one foot long.

The shoreline was fenced to discourage terrestrial based predators. Neither otter nor mink harassed the young Muskies, but their size did not increase.

Disease was not the answer. The corpses of dead fish were not washed up on shore. And no known fish disease was so selective it would attack only fish longer than one foot.

After many years of frustration, a biologist checked the scales of the fish to determine their age. He found the 12-inch Muskies were, consistently, two years old. Smaller fish were older or younger.

Some of the specimens were actually smaller than any of the fingerlings which had been planted! And the smallest of those—less than an inch long—

had scale rings which showed them to be nine years old—the age of the experiment!

This clue led the biologists to an investigation of the fish hatchery where the Muskellunge eggs had hatched. It soon became apparent the Muskie eggs had been fertilized by No-See-Ums.

While the fish grew in Muskie fashion for two years, the No-See-Um addition to their DNA chains then took over and, thereafter, the fish grew smaller and smaller each year.

Fish Managers were faced with a dilemma. They knew old Muskies did not reproduce. They knew old Muskies ate the young of their own species. But they had a 40-inch minimum size limit on the Muskellunge.

If nothing were done, these one-inch Muskies would age to their cannibal stage, attack and eat all of the larger but younger of the species and the Muskellunge fishery would be destroyed.

This explains why, during the 1940's, the Conservation Commission initiated new Muskellunge size limitations. Any Muskie over two inches long had to be thrown back. Only those under two inches long could be kept.

Fishermen, back from the war, flocked to the northern lakes in search of a trophy. When a one-inch Muskie attacked a thirteen-inch plug, during the ensuing battle the plug often threw the Muskie loose into the water. Only the very expert anglers were successful.

The world's record smallest Noseeumuskie measured three eighths of an inch and was landed by a Green Bay tavern owner. It has been mounted as a tie clasp which he proudly displays to customers on special occasions.

Some dishonorable fishermen refused to keep the less-than-two-inch Noseeumuskies and threw them back. But their thoughtless action did no serious damage and the management program was successful.

With no new plantings and the removal of the small trophies, the Noseeumuskie population fell dramatically. Those which were not caught on plugs shrunk to nothingness and disappeared entirely.

No longer under attack by the tiny fish, the Muskellunge prospered. Soon the Conservation Department was able to again impose the 40-inch limitation and the species was preserved.

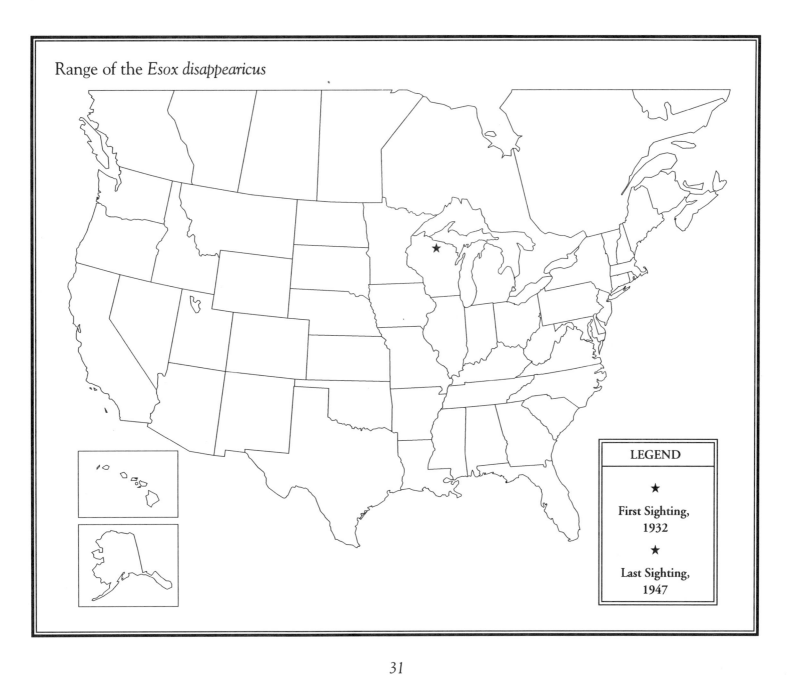

Range of the *Esox disappearicus*

LEGEND

★

First Sighting,
1932

★

Last Sighting,
1947

THE GREAT NORTHERN SNOW SNAKE

(Nordicus albacoilus [venomous])

The Great Northern Snow Snake is easily distinguishable from the Lesser Snow Snake. The former has segments of pure white color separated by inch-long bands of exactly the same pigmentation, while the latter's bands are separated by the segments. And the Lesser Snow Snake is larger than the other one.

The range of the Great Northern Snow Snake extends from the southern shoreline of Lake Superior to the southernmost edges of those forests which are covered by snow between mid November and mid March.

One of the unique characteristics of this reptile is its practice of hibernating during the spring, summer and fall. It awakes from its eight-month sleep only when the ground is covered with snow.

Certain learned expositors claim the snake is imaginary and challenge its defenders to produce one—alive or dead. While unable to produce a specimen, other scientists refer to the accounts of early colonial naturalists who describe the reptile as being, at that time, "cream colored with a few reddish-brown spots scattered about here and there."

These scientists point to the feeding habits of the Wood Tick Hawk which, before its extinction, fed on the Great Northern Snow Snake during the winter. Obviously, the fewer brown spots on the snake, the better its chances to avoid becoming dinner.

The hawks, they opine, killed off all the individuals which had any brown coloration whatsoever. Thus, all presently surviving Great Northern Snow Snakes are of pure white pigmentation.

This gives them excellent camouflage as they move about on or under the snow covered forest floor. It makes them very hard to see. Just because you've never seen or caught one doesn't mean they

don't exist. They're there.

This species of snake is endowed with very poor eyesight—a characteristic which has made Snow Snake reproduction a sometimes thing. When the male seeks out the female during the three-day January mating season, its limited vision, coupled with the perfect camouflage of his intended, ofttimes results in an unsuccessful search.

On other occasions, the cruising male may come across another male. The Great Northern Snow Snake enjoys extensive foreplay. The mating dance, requiring both sexes to stand on the very tips of their tails, is difficult and takes hours to perfect. Much time can be wasted before an error in mate identification is discovered by both parties.

In such cases another two days are lost while the two males extend profuse and protracted apologies, first one to the other, and then the other to the one, and back and forth, forth and back, and so on.

The careful listener who enjoys walking through the waist deep snows of wild and remote northern forests during unbearable subzero temperatures may hear the soft but repetitive sound of "Gnss, Gnss, Gnss" followed, after a short interval, with an answering "Gnss, Gnss, Gnss."

Experts translate that sibilant "gnss" to mean the equivalent of the English "Sorry, old man." They give absolutely no support to the suggestion that the sound has been adopted by the reptile as an acronym of its name.

The bite of the Great Northern Snow Snake is poisonous to anyone over the age of 18 (21 in some states). Medical doctors who claim to know about such things prescribe distilled beverage both as a preventative and as an antidote for the venom.

Herpetologists specializing in the study of the Great Northern Snow Snake fall into three categories. One group claims the snake is extinct. Another claims, though not extinct, the snake's numbers have dwindled to the point that it should be included on the endangered species list. The third think the first two are being silly.

They refer to the snowmobiler fraternity which spends a good deal of time in the woods during that part of the year when the reptile is most active. Snowmobilers recognize the extent of the Snow Snake population as well as the danger of their bite by providing frequent pit stops along their trails where appropriate snow snake venom antidote can be purchased.

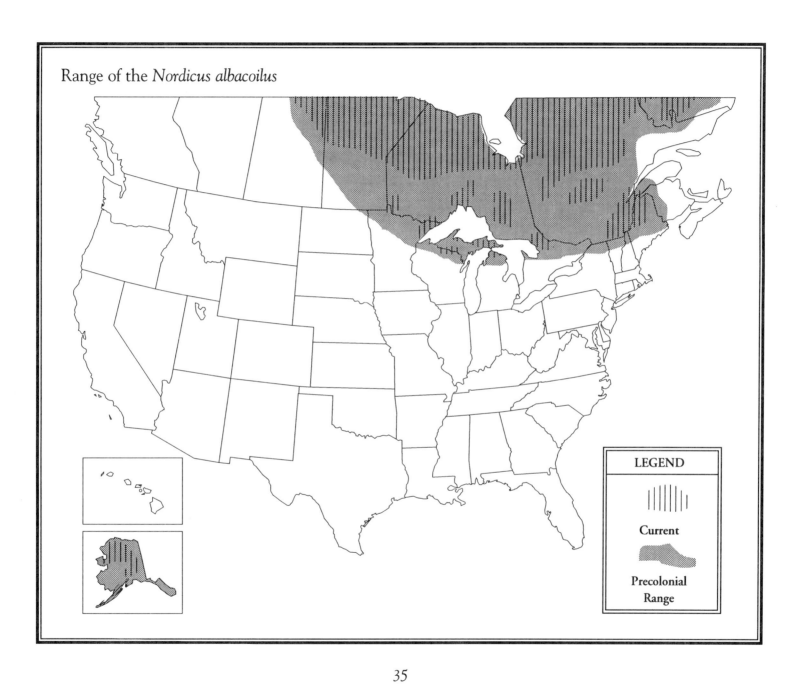

Range of the *Nordicus albacoilus*

LEGEND

Current

Precolonial
Range

THE WOOSE GROCK

(*Wrongwayus invertibuttacus*)

It is time for an authentic and perceptive tract that accurately describes this common but yet largely undefined native of the northern woods.

Early observers have so confused the Woose Grock with the Ruffed Grouse and the Woodcock that their commentaries are, at best, valueless, and in any case, misleading and convoluted.

There is ample reason for that confusion. The female of the species has a long cylindrical beak. It is poked into the soft mud of creek bottoms as the bird searches for its favorite earthworm food. It has a short stubby tail.

The Woose Grock ree is almost universally mistaken for the Woodcock.

The male Woose Grock does not like the ree's cooking and won't eat earthworms. It likes seeds and grasses but will feed on mushroom and even acorns.

It is endowed with both a ruff and a fanned tail. To the casual observer, the male Woose Grock looks remarkably like the Ruffed Grouse.

Scientists presume the bird has learned to read. This theory is accepted by most experts and accounts for the Woose Grock's fervent desire to have nothing to do with the human being.

Many people who have been able to develop a similar ability and who read newspapers—especially the accounts of what is happening in Washington D.C. and in our larger cities—have adopted the same attitude.

Some birds—like eagles—love to pose for the cameraman, looking regal or noble or industrious or merely cute. Not so the Woose Grock. The Woose Grock has no desire to impress anybody and it really doesn't care what you think about it. It strictly avoids association with the human kind, whether

armed with camera, with gun or otherwise.

Apparently the bird is not photogenic. A clear picture of it has never been produced. Hunters have been singularly unsuccessful in taking either the male or the female of the species. Not a single taxidermed specimen has ever become available for study.

The Woose Grock's bodily configuration assists in its interest to disassociate completely with the Homo sapiens. To begin with, the feathers of the bird point backwards.

When the tail of the bird became attached to that part of the body which usually contains the skull, there wasn't enough room up there for the head. So it had to move to the position it now commands—right where the tail should be.

Upland game hunters who wander the autumn forests easily recognize the Woose Grock. Sightings are common. But, much to the disgust of good pointing dogs, they have been unable to bag the bird.

When the Woose Grock is in flight, its backwards construction leads the hunter to believe the bird is moving 180 degrees away from the actual line of its flight. This induces them to lead the bird in the wrong direction and, as a consequence, they always miss it.

Hunters report the call of the Woose Grock is heard only after explosions—like gun shots—and sounds like: EEOOOMISSSSDMEE, EEOOOMISS-DMEE, EEOOMISSDMEE.

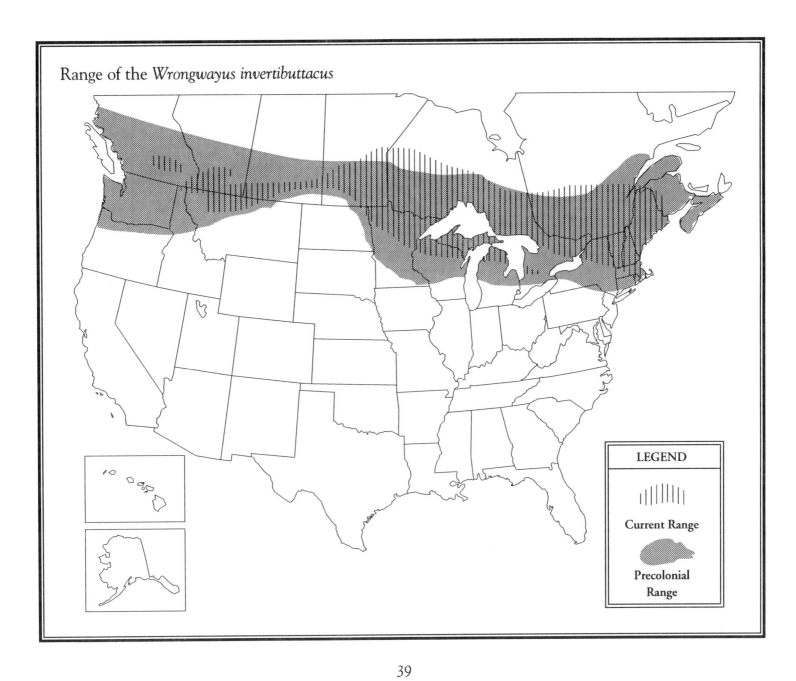

Range of the *Wrongwayus invertibuttacus*

LEGEND

Current Range

Precolonial Range

NOCH LESS MONSTER

(Hangoverus maximus)

Rumors of the existence of strange creatures trapped in freshwater lakes have long fascinated and attracted the attentions of fishermen, anthropologists and other peculiar people.

Most of the reported sightings are not substantiated by credible evidence, and the very existence of those aquatic beasts is suspect and subject to serious question. Many cases have been proven to be fraudulent or the product of a disturbed mind.

An example of the latter is Scotland's famed Loch Ness Monster. Though submarine equipment, sonar, modern electronic devices and megabucks (probably secured through some U.S. Congressional grant) have been employed in the search, no definitive conclusions or proof of the monster's existence were obtained—until last month.

A Scottish teetotaler (himself an endangered species in the Highland country) discovered that the first sighting of the Loch Ness Monster occurred simultaneously with the initial production of Scotch drinking whisky by the distillery which had established itself on the shore of the lake.

Still, the existence of some of these legendary animals is supported by solid evidence and, to many, proven beyond the shadow of the doubt. The Noch Less Monster falls into this category.

Little is known about this illusive animal. It is well established that it lives in northern lakes, streams and rivers that contain concentrations of aquatic life. Presumably, it is a fish eater.

Another salient but peculiar characteristic of the beast is its ability to swim only an inch or two below the surface of the water at rapid speeds but without leaving any wake or other indication whatsoever of its movement.

It is also known that the Noch Less Monster has

a penchant for kidnapping human beings. Case histories prove its kidnappings are limited to male, married fishermen—and no one else.

In fact, the first verified report of the existence of the monster came from a fisherman. The monster had held him captive for eight full days before he was able to escape.

Such kidnappings are common and continue to occur on northern lakes. The victims suffer no apparent injury or harm—excepting, sometimes, a temporary disorder which behaves suspiciously like a hangover.

The kidnappings do, however, delay the return of the fisherman to his home. And sometimes fishing companions feel it is necessary to remain at the lake to search for and, if possible, secure the safe release of the unfortunate victim.

Extensive studies show the Noch Less Monster involves itself in abductions only when the fishing is good.

Wives are generally relieved and pleased when a kidnappee returns unscathed from the terrifying experience. But recently a suspicious spouse questioned the kidnapping—and this in spite of the supporting statements made by the husband's fishing companion who was present and witnessed the entire affair.

Luckily the companion had taken his camera. He produced a photograph which allayed the baseless suspicions of the lady. The photo was of excellent quality and clearly showed a large portion of the lake and a wide stretch of shoreline. Not a single ripple appears on the water—thus incontrovertibly proving the presence of the wakeless Noch Less Monster.

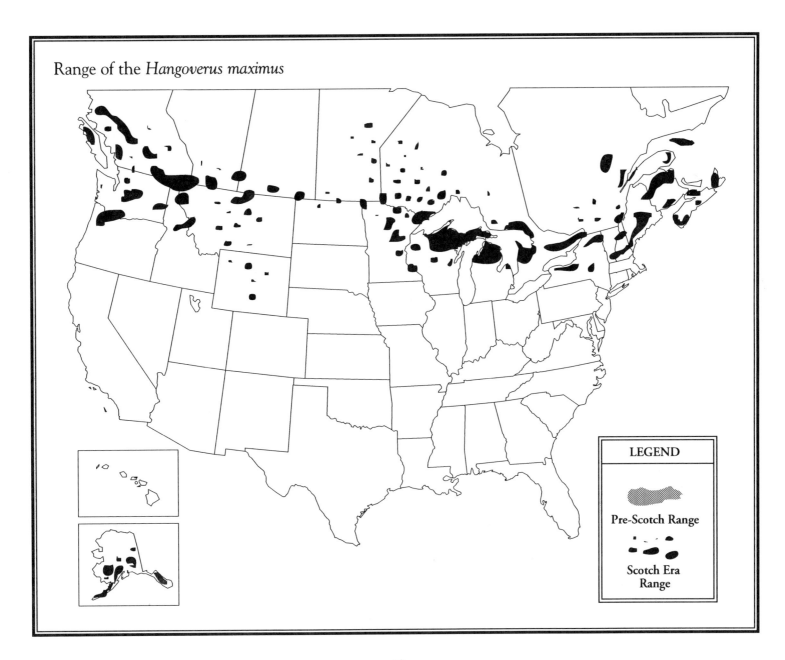

Range of the *Hangoverus maximus*

LEGEND

Pre-Scotch Range

Scotch Era Range

THE WOODTICK HAWK

(Dambugis irritatus)

In precolonial times the Woodtick Hawk had not evolved. In those days this bird was indistinguishable from the Chicken Hawk. But since domestic chickens had not yet been introduced to the North American continent, the Chicken Hawks had a tough time of it.

One group of them, astutely recognizing the basic problem and being unhappy with the constant battle to keep from starving, as well as the appearance of the lady hawks (universally as skinny and unattractive as Paris models), began the practice of eating woodticks.

Over the centuries they built a taste for the insects, and their migration patterns reflected their search for only this kind of food. In the fall of the year when the woodtick population dropped in the northern limits of their territories, the Woodtick Hawk would migrate to the south where ticks remained active.

This pattern changed when the birds' search for food brought them into what is now Northern Michigan—an area which is still recognized for its mammoth concentrations of huge, fat ticks.

Over the years, as they continued to enjoy the plentiful supply of foodstuff represented by the Michigan Woodticks, the hawks grew larger and larger. And as they became fatter and fatter, their migratory flights became more and more difficult.

Ultimately the birds got so big they could no longer fly and had to walk on the annual autumnal southern journeys. This took them through Detroit. The pollution, muggings and gunshots they experienced there soon convinced them to give up migrations altogether.

Tick politicians called Town Hall meetings and convinced Hawkdom that fat, accumulated during

the spring and summer, would allow the birds to survive through the tickless winter season. But to be on the safe side, they called in experts to instruct the hawks on how to store excess foods for consumption during lean periods.

The squirrels gave the hawks good advice. The Hawks adopted the practice of establishing caches of woodticks in hollow trees and in holes in the ground. But the hawks refused to consider the recommendation that they adopt the policy of semihibernations during the colder times of year.

The hawks claimed it was unbirdlike and contrary to their cultural history.

Their absolute refusal to adapt, particularly with regard to hibernation and to food preference, seriously endangered the Woodtick Hawk's ability to survive. When any imbalance in nature disrupts the food source, that species faces extinction. Such was the case of the Woodtick Hawk.

Some birds belatedly tried to adapt. They decided to eat snow snakes. But since the reptiles were white and superbly camouflaged, they were an inadequate food source. At the end of the second winter, all Woodtick Hawks had starved to death.

Yes, the Woodtick Hawk is considered to be as extinct as the Saber-Toothed Tiger—which suffered the same fate which overtakes any species when its limited food supply disappears. (The Saber-Toothed Tiger fed only on honest politicians.)

Reports of huge walking birds continue to be heard. They come mostly from Upper Michigan. Yooper doctors referred to such reports as: "Da Tickhawk Syndrome." Medical science, using its acronymical shorthand, calls it "the DTs."

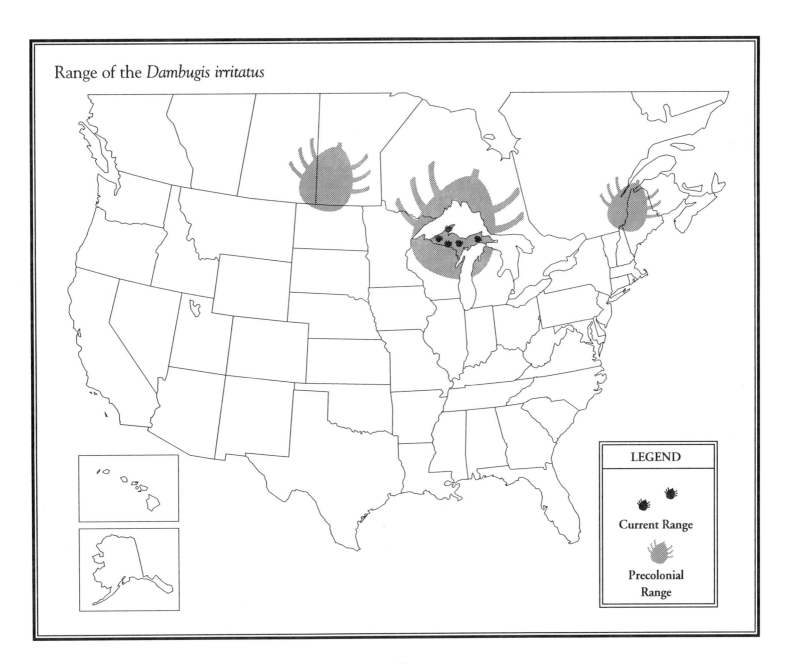

Range of the *Dambugis irritatus*

LEGEND

Current Range

Precolonial Range

THE ANTLERED BROWN TROUT

(Salmo trutta frutta)

The *Salmo trutta* is a native of Europe and some parts of Asia and Africa. It was introduced into the United States in 1883. At present, German Brown Trout (as they are technically known) are found from New Zealand to Bolivia, from India to Patagonia, from Venezuela to Madagascar—in almost every part of the world where there are cold water streams—excepting only Antarctica.

Professor Norbert Hefflefinger attributes the thriving populations and wide geographic distribution of the fish to the female Brown Trout's cute smile and entertaining wiggle. Most fish biologists claim it is because the *Salmo trutta* has a highly developed ability to adapt and is of very aggressive temperament.

Those characteristics explain the development of the fish into its most spectacular mutation—the *Salmo trutta frutta*, or Antlered Brown Trout.

As the German Brown made its way into northern forest streams, it chased suckers, carp, the northern crocodile and other forms of aquatic life from the waters. Without such competition, the fish rapidly increased in size. Caddis, Green Drakes and other insect life did not satisfy its voracious appetite. It added frogs to its diet.

The fish became even bigger and sought still more and larger foods to supply its growing needs. Soon muskrats and beavers began to disappear from rivers. Hunters reported chasing deer into streams and watching, in horror, as the animals were eaten by schools of the fish in piranha-attack fashion. Theorists claim the *Salmo trutta frutta* developed from such incidents.

When it began to feed on mammals and digest their bones, the *Salmo trutta* suddenly ingested large

49

amounts of calcium. Since the fish's bony structure is delicate, very little of that mineral is needed or found in its usual diet. The calcium turned most animal-eating German Browns stiffer than a board and they floated to the surface, as dead as mackerel.

(When you see huge Browns mounted on cabin walls, check them carefully for calcium deposits. Many fishermen are liars and will claim catching them when, in fact, they found them amid the shore debris after the springtime high water receded. They simply nailed them to boards and hung them on the wall.)

Other German Browns, however, noticing the antlers on the deer they devoured, elected to rid themselves of the excess calcium by sprouting horns. And thus the *Salmo trutta frutta* or Antlered Brown Trout subspecies came into being.

The first reports of the Antlered Brown Trout came from a Lake Winnipeg winter fisherman. He was in his shack beside a 3 by 4 foot hole in the ice, waiting for a northern to swim by. He reported a horned beast leaped from the water, ripped the spear from his hand and chased him out onto the open ice.

Since he was a drinker, his story was considered a figment of an overlubricated imagination.

Deer hunters, on the other hand, witnessing the antlered fish attacking deer, became intrigued. They returned to the rivers when they were frozen over and drilled observation holes though the ice. Soon they discovered the runways of the Antlered Brown Trout.

When the trout season opened, the hunters, armed with both deer tags and fishing permits, returned to the haunts of the fish, successfully caught a few specimens and established the existence of the creature.

Dry-fly fishermen use forty-pound tippet and claim the fish will rise to take live pheasants, if properly presented.

(There have been recent disturbing developments. Unscrupulous poachers have trained dogfish to chase the *Salmo trutta frutta* and herd it into shallow shoals were they are shot with .30.30 rifles.)

Range of the *Salmo trutta frutta*

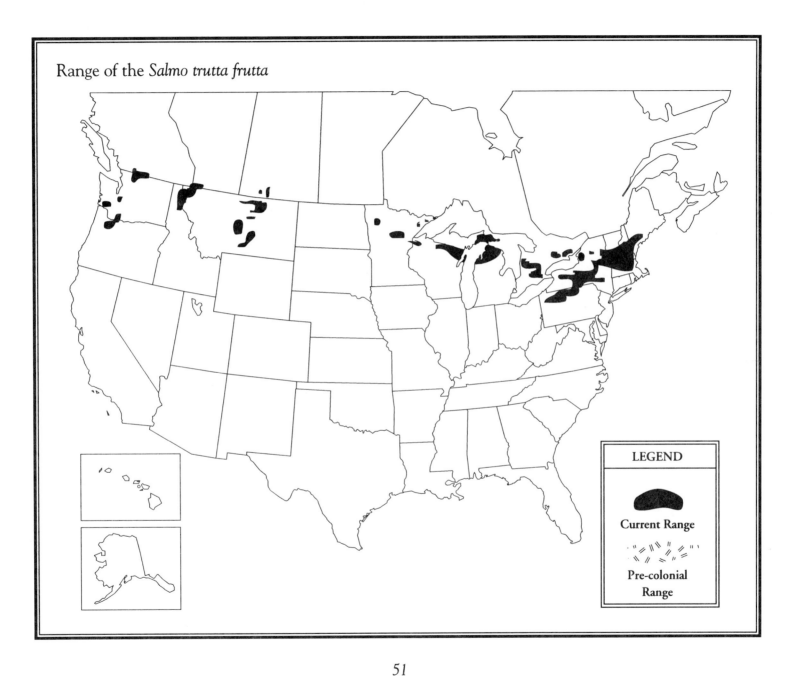

LEGEND

Current Range

Pre-colonial
Range

THE WHITETAIL DEER

(Odocoileus virginianis borealis)

Norbert Hefflefinger was born and raised in Chicago. He received his Ph.D. from Northwestern University. His doctoral thesis was the much acclaimed *"Rattus chicagoensis hauspetis—A study of the Ecology of Urban Sewers."*

For the past seven years, Professor Hefflefinger has studied the *Odocoileus virginianis borealis*, or, as it is more commonly called, the Northern Virginia or Whitetail Deer.

We are indeed fortunate to have the Professor's authorization to reprint the following quotation from his as yet unpublished study, "The Genus Odocoileus."

"It has usually been assumed the present representatives of the Northern Virginia Deer family emerged during the Pleistocene epoch. It is interesting to note no qualified writer claims there is any direct relationship between the Whitetail and the deer of the Old World.

"Many authorities claim, due to excellent habitat and population management, there are now more Whitetail Deer in the United States than ever before in history.

"Well, I'm here to tell you the Whitetail Deer is a mythical beast an' don't you let anyone tell you any different.

"I been huntin 'em for seven–eight years now an' I ain't never seen one of 'em. I hunt hard, too.

"I git out there early. Then I take my two-face ax an' go around cuttin' brush an' branches for to build a blind. I carry my gun with me too, 'cause I was told if you don't have a gun with you that's when they'll come at you. Every time.

"It takes more 'n an hour to get a good blind built, an' I carry my gun, too, but I don't see no deer when I'm building it. Once I built a real good blind.

It was a dandy. But it was so good I couldn't see outen it, so I din't see no Whitetail Deer that time neither.

"Once I git my blind built, I wait maybe ten minutes an' if nothin' comes along I figure maybe I'm not in the right place, so I move to another likely spot and build another blind.

"I do that a lot so I cover a lot of good deer country, but I ain't never seen a deer. Not one.

"Yes sir, the *Odocoileus virginianis borealis* is sure legendary or—if it ever was—it's extinct now."

Range of the *Odocoileus virginianis borealis*

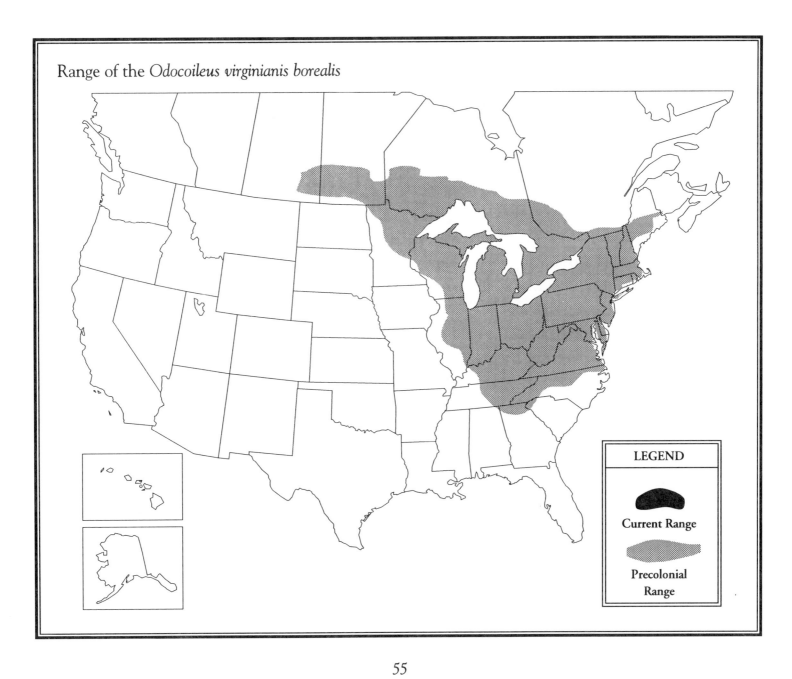

LEGEND

Current Range

Precolonial
Range

55

THE SMALLFOOT

(Ursus micropodia)

Scientists unanimously agree the Smallfoot is in no way related to either of its cousins, the Himalayan Yeti (a/k/a the Abominable Snowman) or the Pacific Northwest Sasquatch (a/k/a the Bigfoot).

The main reason for that attitude is the undeniable fact that neither Bigfoot nor the Abominable Snowman have convinced themselves they actually exist, whereas the Smallfoot has no question about the matter.

The Sasquatch and the Yeti both walk upright and look ugly—like troglodytes or Neanderthals. They have big feet. The Smallfoot usually walks on all fours and, by comparison, looks lovely—just like a black bear. The species are further distinguished by the hitherto unrecognized fact that the Smallfoot has small feet.

The tracks of even the adult Smallfoot are nearly indistinguishable from the footprints of a small boy, say six or seven years old. Early investigators of the Smallfoot were often frustrated by this fact. Their diaries would contain notations like: "Spent another day looking for the Smallfoot. Couldn't find a thing—only the track of some small barefooted boy."

Even today, with the existence of the Smallfoot confirmed and its special pedal characteristic well known, a similar but reverse kind of confusion is sometimes evident, like when a small boy is lost and the people looking for him discover the prints of his bare feet but don't follow them. The poor lad dies of exposure simply because the searchers think his tracks are those of the Smallfoot.

Since the Smallfoot feeds exclusively on Brook Trout, it is seldom seen in urban areas, and only then in restaurants which specialize in the preparation of freshwater fish.

The most recent sightings of the Smallfoot occurred on the Stanley Jagow farm—more specifically, along the banks of Jagow Creek (locally referred to as Stan's Creek). Stan's Creek runs through sand country, and it was along its banks that the characteristic small-boy footprints were first seen.

There were no youngsters in the vicinity and the presence of the Smallfoot was immediately suspected. Unfortunately the excellent trout population of Stan's Creek attracted trout fishermen as well as the Smallfoot, and one of them, believing it to be a bear, shot and killed it.

The trout fisherman noticed the peculiar feet of the animal. This excited his curiosity. He thought they were caused by some sort of rare bear genetic defect. He had his camera with him so he took a picture to be able to prove his story about the bear with the funny looking feet.

When he discovered he had the only known photo of a Smallfoot, he sent it to a noted outdoor artist. He commissioned an oil painting showing the animal and the location on Stan's Creek where it had been taken.

When the painting was finished, the artist inadvertently destroyed the photograph. The painting is now exhibited at the Neopolitan Museum of Art in Iron River, Michigan. It shows the Smallfoot in the foreground and Jagow's Creek gently flowing behind it. The painting is entitled: "Boy-Foot Bear with Creek of Stan."

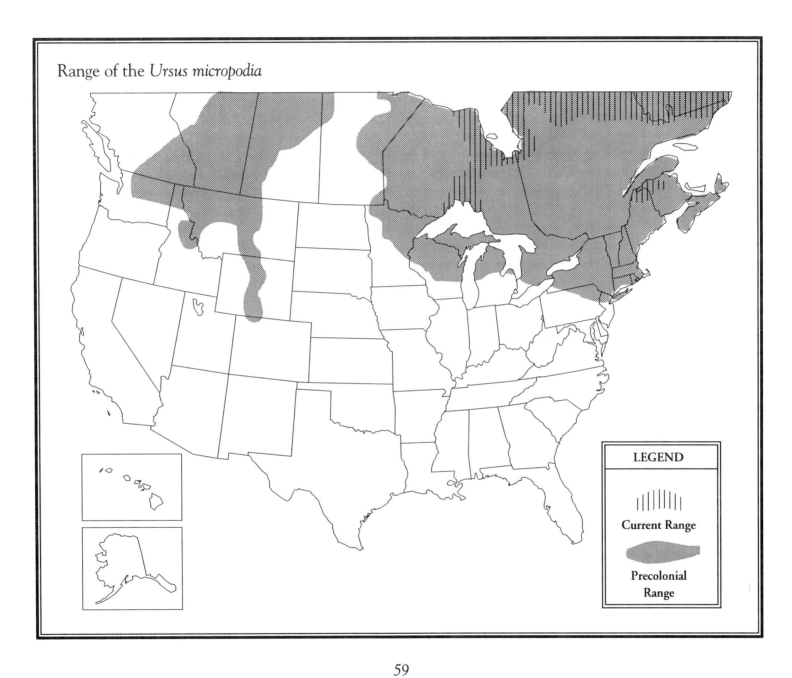

Range of the *Ursus micropodia*

LEGEND

Current Range

Precolonial Range

THE LUMBERJACK PARROT

(Vocalus alertis)

Working in the woods from sunup to sundown and sharpening axes and saws occupied most of the lumberjack's time. The balance of his leisure was spent eating, sleeping and tending to the needs of the horses upon which his employment depended.

He had little time to spare for the care and maintenance of any other domestic animal. For this reason, lumberjack pets tended to be wild animals, capable of fending for themselves.

Porcupines, mice, weasels, lice, Canada Jays (the "Camp Robber") and other non-hibernating animals are common examples. Many such creatures took up residence close to lumberjacks simply because logging camps were an excellent source of food.

Other than providing companionship, few such creatures performed any positive function for the men. For the most part, they were nothing more than nuisances.

The porcupines chewed up the ax handles for salt, the mice changed wheat flour into buckwheat flour, and the weasels smelled up the place. The Lumberjack Parrot, however, was an exception.

This bird had no destructive habits and performed many valuable services for the lumberjack, the first of which was recognized as a consequence of the bird's customary nesting procedures. Prior to retiring for the evening, it would call its mate— which had been out shopping or gadding about.

The call would occur precisely one-half hour before sundown and took the form of the sound: "Tiee, Tiee, Tiee, Tiee." As this cry echoed throughout the woods, the men, believing it to be the cook telling them it was time for supper, would immediately head back to camp.

When they discovered it was the parrot (and not the cook's yelling of "Time, Time, Time, Time"), they gave it the camp name of "Time Bird" and began to feed and tame it. Soon the parrot was performing other useful functions in the logging operations.

The bottoms of the feet of the Lumberjack Parrot were particularly nubbly. This allowed the bird to land and hold onto ice covered branches without slipping. The fact did not go unnoticed by the loggers. The origin of hobnail boots is, thus, attributed to this parrot.

As in the case of most members of the parrot family, the configuration of the bird's tongue and its native intelligence were soon evident. It learned to speak.

In the 1880's, working in the woods was a dangerous occupation. The most perilous hazard was that of being struck by a falling tree. The incidence of squashed lumberjacks was common. Broken arms and legs were a familiar occupational occurrence.

As the Lumberjack Parrot became dependent upon and bonded to his human friend, it would accompany him to the cutting areas and warn him of impending injury.

As a huge pine began to fall, the parrot's loud cries of "Look out, you idiot" saved the life of many a man who otherwise would have been flattened by a tree one of his companions or he himself had cut.

By the 1890's the value of the Lumberjack Parrot was so recognized, the sawyers would seek its warning cries by calling out to it whenever a tree they cut was about to fall. Their cries of "Time Bird, Time Bird" eventually changed into "Timber, Timber"— the falling tree warning still given today.

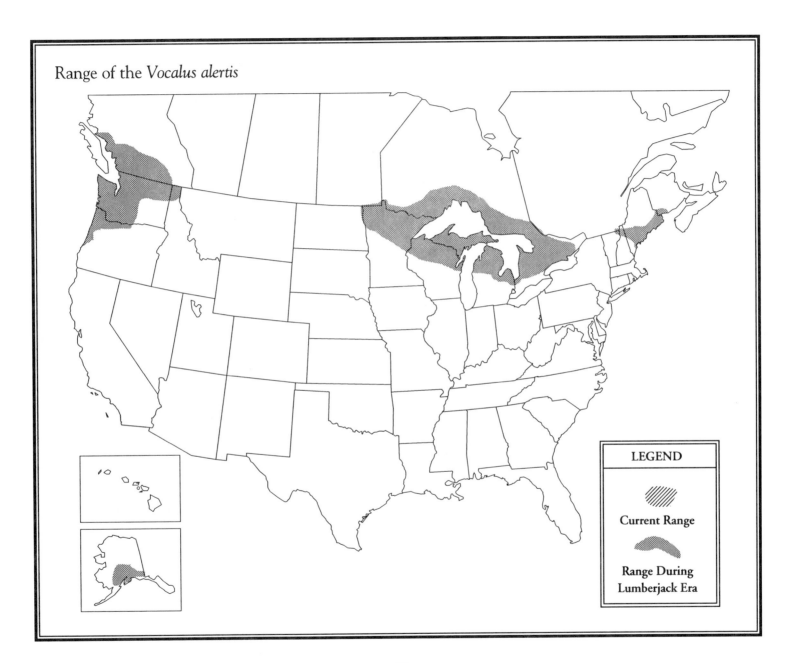

Range of the *Vocalus alertis*

LEGEND

Current Range

Range During
Lumberjack Era

THE HOOP SNAKE

(*Rollatum hystericus*)

Since its first sighting in the 1880s, the Hoop Snake has generated considerable interest and commentary in the scientific community.

Early naturalists considered this snake to be a vicious, irritable and aggressive reptile. These accounts were undoubtedly occasioned by the reports of terrified lumberjacks who, believing they were under attack, panicked and ran when they saw the Hoop Snake wheeling down hills at them.

Modern investigators are convinced the creature actually was of a mild and peaceful nature. And, as one of the more delicious and nourishing members of its genus, all forest predators recognized the Hoop Snake as a good meal. Thus, constantly in danger of assault and unable to defend itself with either fang or venom, the snake's only manner of defense was flight.

To develop more speed when threatened, the Hoop Snake would bite the tip of its own tail, raise itself upright into a spokeless wheel and careen down hills to safety. This accounts for the reptile's preference for hilltop habitat and exposes the timorous lumberjacks' slander of the good name and character of the Hoop Snake.

This manner of defense became genetically imprinted. Over the years, the head of the snake became permanently affixed to the tail. The two parts so successfully melded together, only a careful search would reveal the two small black eyes indicating the location of the head. This physical configuration made feeding difficult.

Scientists are still engaged in developing theories to determine and explain the reptile's eating habits. And as soon as they have solved that riddle, they'll embark on a second and equally important investigation—i.e., How did the snake evacuate fully processed foodstuffs?

Unfortunately, this placid and gentle creature is now extinct. Its demise as a species occurred during the fifty-year period surrounding the turn of the last century.

In the 1880s, when the existence of Hoop Snakes was first reported, certain unscrupulous coopers began trapping them for commercial purposes. They put the snakes in pens and bred them. This trapping and domestication of the reptile was economically driven and the practice was commonly adopted in coopers' circles. The trapping became so widespread the number of wild Hoop Snakes declined precipitously. Sightings became rare, and then stopped completely. The last wild Hoop was seen in 1910. Thereafter only domesticated Hoop Snakes were extant. The specter of extinction had not yet threatened them. They filled the coopers' pens.

In midwinter, when the Hoop Snake was hibernating and rigidly frozen in its circular form, the coopers, during their barrel construction processes, would slide the snakes down over the wooden staves and use them as substitutes for the more expensive iron barrel hoops.

After the barrels had been sold, and in the spring when the warming breezes arrived, the snakes would thaw out and wiggle loose from their retaining positions. The barrel, of course, would collapse into a pile of staves.

Upon discovering the presence of a Hoop Snake and noting its circular construction, the owners of collapsed barrels presumed the snake had eaten the iron hoops. It is easy to see why, in their ignorance, they would order the peremptory killing of the Hoop Snake. Then they'd order another barrel.

This is precisely what the coopers had in mind. Economists point to these last-century practices of barrel makers as the first known example of planned obsolescence.

After the conclusion of World War I, metal drums largely replaced wooden barrels and the cooper's trade fell upon bad times. Facing bankruptcy, the manufacturers of wooden barrels simply turned the Hoop Snakes loose to fend for themselves and abandoned their businesses.

But the Hoop Snakes had been so long domesticated they were unable to adjust to the vicissitudes of life in the wild and fell easy prey to the dreaded snake-eating mouse.

This gentle snake was soon declared extinct—a victim of modern technology.

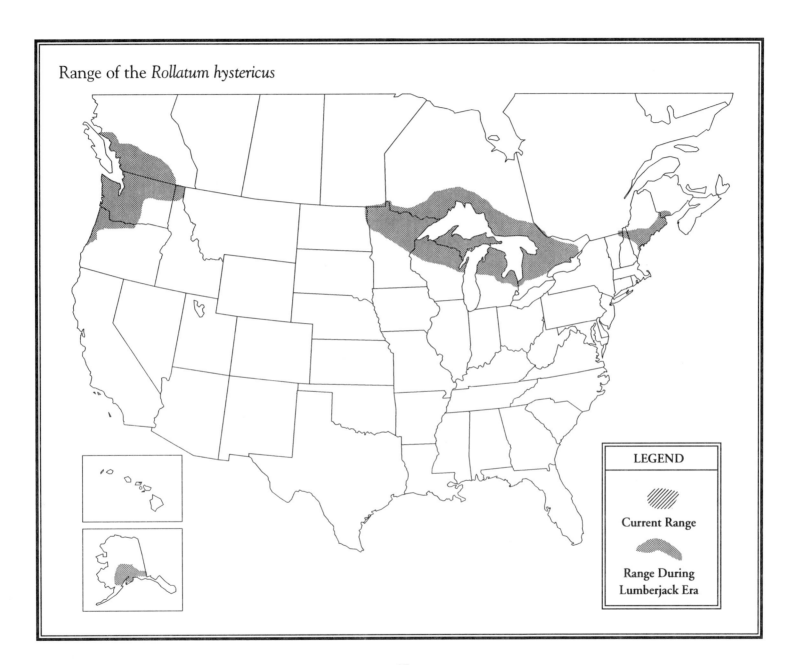

Range of the *Rollatum hystericus*

LEGEND

Current Range

Range During
Lumberjack Era

THE GIANT MANTIS

(Juris preyuponus)

We owe the discovery of the existence of the Giant Mantis to a practicing attorney and not to field biologists.

The story begins in 1920 when the McCall & McGhee Lumber Company purchased two sections of forest land. The property was located inside a huge stand of virgin white pine. The company commenced its logging operation and the cutting and hauling proceeded without remarkable incident.

In 1923, the owner of the sections adjacent to the McCall & McGhee properties brought suit for timber trespass. He claimed the company had logged not only its own two sections but had cut four adjoining forties of prime quality white pine forest belonging to him. He demanded treble damages.

The logging company vehemently denied the charges and hired an attorney to defend its interests. A survey was commissioned. It confirmed the allega-tion that four forties not belonging to McCall & McGhee (but adjacent thereto) had, in fact, been clearcut.

The only logging roads in the area ran through the company's property, and local residents swore the sound of axe had not been heard nor had any logging activity taken place since McCall & McGhee had left.

With this evidence adduced, the complainant attorney rested his case, and it was evident the jury was favorably impressed by the proofs. It looked bad for McCall & McGhee.

The company's legal counsel was not intimi-dated. He convinced the jury his client had not improperly cut the neighbor's trees.

The Preying Mantis was well known to everyone in the courtroom. When the company lawyer got through, the jury was equally aware of the Giant Mantis.

The attorney gave the jury a full and accurate description of that northwoods creature together with its characteristic lifestyle. His reports were so complete and accurate, no further investigation or research was deemed necessary for the preparation of this portion of this text.

All of the following information comes from the court reporter's record of the argument to the jury in the McCall & McGhee case.

The Giant Mantis shares a number of characteristics with its distant cousin, the Preying Mantis.

Both have the ability to remain motionless for long periods of time—the Preying Mantis for up to a half hour as it waits for its prey to approach.

As reported by the attorney for McCall & McGhee, the Giant Mantis, with its low metabolism, is able to remain motionless for such long periods that it actually becomes a part of its environment.

The Giant Mantis is a timid and retiring creature. It does not like loud noises—like those heard during logging operations. Entire colonies of Giant Mantis have been known to leave an area when they occur.

When the Giant Mantis has become attached to its surroundings, it must first cut itself off at the ankles before it can migrate to different territory. It accomplishes this maneuver by a rapid twisting motion. This leaves a stump which might be easily mistaken for one left after a sawyer has fallen a tree.

Both Preying and Giant Mantis are masters of disguise, endowed by nature with a camouflage that hides them from all but the most discerning eye. The attorney informed the jury that the Giant Mantis can so well adopt the color and form of its surroundings that its presence had only been recently discovered.

He further informed them the Giant Mantis looks exactly like a white pine.

The company's attorney was very good. Very expensive, but very good.

Even today, the camouflage abilities of the Giant Mantis are so well developed that environmentalists are unable to locate them. We can report no more than the presumption that the Giant Mantis population is thriving somewhere in the northern forests, and the species is not endangered.

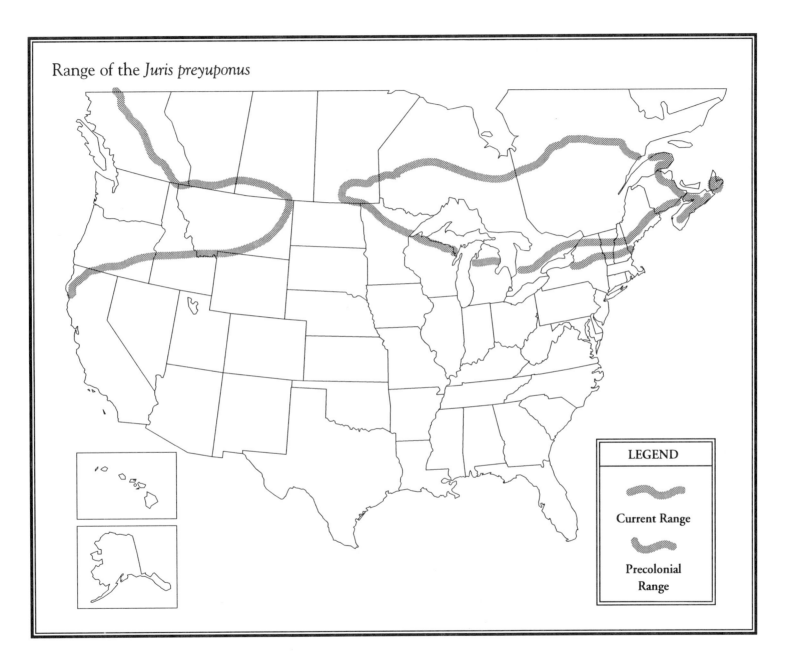

Range of the *Juris preyuponus*

LEGEND

Current Range

Precolonial
Range

OCTODOG

(Octocanis borealis)

Until recently natural history text books referred to it only as "The Unknown Creature." This was because very little was known about it. Reports of the creature were almost as numerous as those of the flying saucer—but not nearly as probable, nor from such credible sources.

To begin with, the thing had never really been seen. Sketchy reports of hearing it rapidly scurrying away through the canopy of the summer forest were all the naturalist had to work with.

Neither the animal nor its tracks had ever been discovered on the ground. Apparently it hibernated before the autumn leaves fell from the trees. (Some learned expositors thought it might have been a night migrator who liked to leave before the crowd arrived in Florida.)

Early naturalists erroneously believed it was related to the Madagascar Lemur which with its prehensile tail could also quickly and easily move through the forest treetops.

We are indebted to Professor Norbert Hefflefinger, whose attentive field work and acute analysis have, at last, removed the mystery surrounding this creature. Professor Hefflefinger's attention was first drawn to this animal during his field trips in study of the Whitetail Deer. He heard the creature moving rapidly through the treetops. He got a government grant and began to study it.

After years of never seeing one, the professor thought it might be related to the deer, but he confirmed the animal never left the forest canopy.

Hefflefinger theorized the animal never came to ground because it had no legs. With impeccable logic he pointed to the example of fish—which have no legs and are seldom seen walking around on the forest floor.

The next phase in the analysis of the creature showed the typical intellectual capacity which characterizes the professor's work.

"Ya," thought Norbert, "that Lemur thing can go fast through the trees. An' he got four legs an' a tail he can use. This thing don't got no legs, but he moves so fast nobody sees 'im. Must be he got more 'n five tails. Six ain't enough. Let's make it eight."

The scientific community immediately went into action. Papers appeared in the leading journals. Some claimed the unknown creature really had eight legs—not tails—and was, therefore, a huge spider.

The Professor clarified matters with further brilliant deduction: "If it was a big ugly spider, where's the spider webs, smart alec?" he queried.

Some claimed the eight appendages marked the creature as an octopus. Others claimed Hefflefinger must have been drinking again.

Hefflefinger easily disposed of the octopus suggestion. If the octopus were once a forest dwelling creature, he reasoned, what could have induced it to leave the land for a home in the sea?

And if the unknown creature were in fact an octopus, why, he wondered, wasn't it hiding in ancient amphorae in the Aegean Sea with its friends, or frightening Victor Hugo heroes?

The professor's conclusions settled the matter once and for all. Though both the octopus and the unknown creature were originally terrestrial animals, there was no common ancestor. The octopus (originally spelled "octo puss") was a mutant of the feline family. The unknown creature sprang from canine antecedents.

Undoubtedly the two species fought like cats and dogs, and apparently the unknown creature so harassed the octo puss that it sought refuge in the sea. It lost the ability to live on land—and one "s" from its name.

In order to avoid any possible erroneous classification of the unknown creature within the octopus family, since the date of publication of the Hefflefinger paper, the unknown creature has been known as the Octodog.

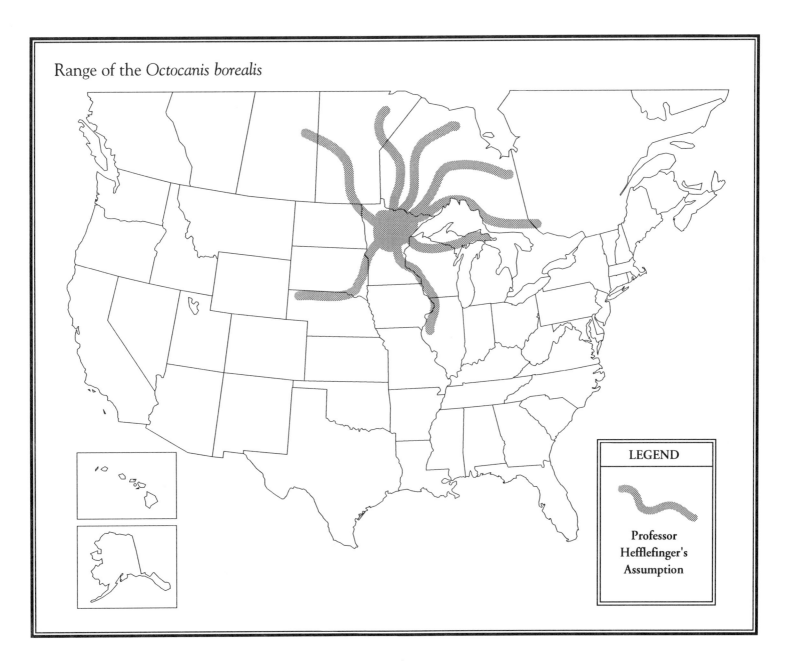

Range of the *Octocanis borealis*

LEGEND

Professor
Hefflefinger's
Assumption

THE OGNIB AND THE ONISAC

(Reservatica gambelon)

No treatise of legendary animals would be complete without reference to those two celebrated protective spirits of the northern Native American tribes—the Ognib and the Onisac.

Either and both of these creatures were charged with the responsibility of coming to the aid of the tribe in the event it ever was in serious trouble and urgently needed help. Prominently featured in woodland Indian lore, both spirits could take the form of any living creature.

During those times when the winters were cold and the beaver few, the Ognib might appear in the form of deer and provide sustenance for the starving tribe. The Onisac frequently assumed the guise of the Diaphanous Moose and inobtrusively watched over the welfare of the tribe.

European settlers, when first informed of the Ognib and Onisac, asked the Indians for specimens of the two creatures. They were sometimes given a porcupine, sometimes a striped skunk and sometimes a Rockworm. The early reports peremptorily dismissed the Ognib and the Onisac as figments of wild imaginations.

Subsequently, scientists, unable to classify them in any single genus, presumed the colonial reports were accurate and for some time thereafter no studies of either of the animals were considered.

During the last half century, however, further research was undertaken. Investigators first proposed and then substantially proved many creatures previously thought to be of fable or fiction do, in fact, exist.

And the ability to assume a different form is now recognized as commonplace. The caterpillar changes into a butterfly. Another example is Santa Claus. He has metamorphosed and now appears in the

character of federal government agencies.

The parallel between the form-changing Santa Claus and the legend of Ognib and Onisac were too close to be ignored. Grants were secured, research programs were launched, and the existence of the two Indian benefactors has been incontrovertibly established.

Inquiries made of Indian folklorists and historians showed the ancient beliefs had nearly been lost as the tribes left their old ways and adopted the strange newer cultures of the European.

This perhaps accounts for the reason help was not forthcoming during past periods of Indian need. The old beliefs had been forsaken. The tribes neglected to ask the spirits for the assistance which was readily available.

During the 1970's and 80's when the tribes suffered from high unemployment, Ognib and Onisac were rediscovered. Senior pagan members taught the ancient Ognib and Onisac dances to the youngsters. Through appropriate ceremony, the intervention of both spirits was earnestly petitioned.

In order to provide comfortable housing for the two creatures, in whatever form they may have decided to reappear, great structures were built. And to make sure they did not become lost or enter into the wrong building, large neon signs carrying both names were erected.

Soon thereafter great numbers of people came to the buildings to worship the two woodland creatures. They offered up large sums of money for advancing the economic well-being of the tribes.

Though no one has as of yet discovered the particular form assumed by Ognib and Onisac when they again manifested themselves, there is no doubt these two powerful spirits have made their appearance and have answered the entreaties of the tribes.

And all this in spite of the fact that a dyslexic employee, when creating the neon signs erected at the large buildings, spelled the names of the two spirits backwards.

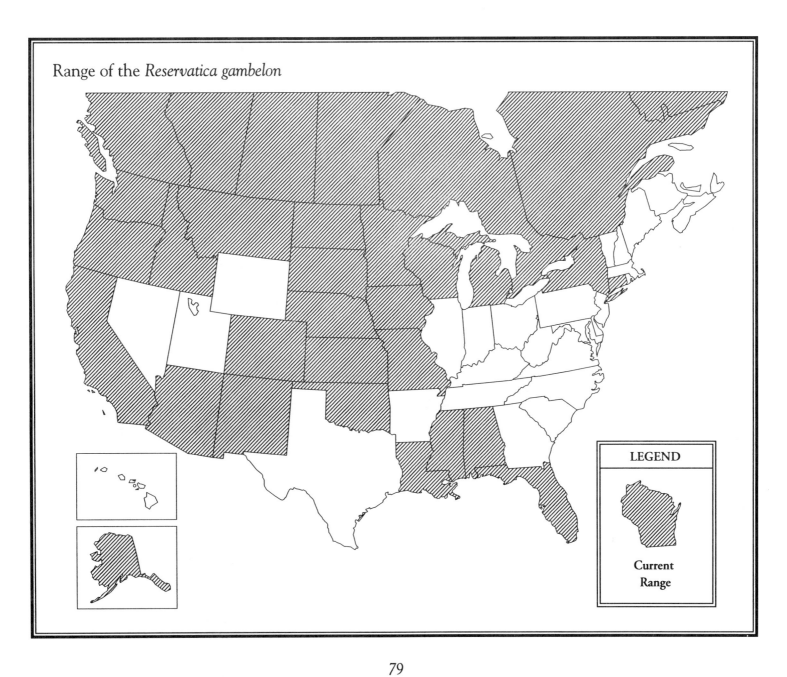

Range of the *Reservatica gambelon*

LEGEND

Current
Range

THE BLUNT-BILLED ROCKPECKER

(Rhinoblunta boulderbanger)

Like the army ants of the Amazon Basin, foraging Canadian Rockworms would, ultimately, destroy all stones found in their path. Left unchecked, they could have destroyed every rock in the northwoods as they pursued their migration to the south and west.

Lord knows what would have happened had they not been stopped. Long lines of stones and boulders advancing through the countryside—sometimes at a rate of speed approaching half an inch a week—would have terrorized and panicked the people.

Theorists speculate the Iowa and Nebraska cattle and corn industries would never have developed. Those rich farmlands would have been rendered sterile by the thick covering of fine silicone droppings left by the marauding, rock encased, slowly but relentlessly advancing worms.

The Rocky Mountains themselves would probably have suffered the same fate as the once magnificent Occidental Sacramento Range of New Mexico. It was completely leveled by a marauding band of Mexican Rockworms and is now known as the White Sands National Monument.

Fortunately, the only natural enemy of the Canadian Rockworm, the Blunt-Billed Rockpecker, made its appearance and not only halted the Rockworm population explosion, but reduced its numbers to such an extent that it no longer poses a threat to our enjoyment of the natural beauty that surrounds all of us who live in the woodland country.

(If you happen to live in a city with a population of over 25,000, send fifty cents to the publisher, plus $9.50 to cover postage and handling. He will send you an immature Rockworm, complete with housing rock. Turn it loose in your backyard or city park and hope for the best. Maybe they'll eat the downtown

cement and bricks and destroy the place.)

(If you happen to be the mayor of a city with a population of over 25,000, you may find your buildings crumbling and a fine white dust settling on the downtown streets. Send 50 cents to the publisher, together with $9.50 to cover shipping and handling, and he will send you a Blunt-Billed Rockpecker egg. When it hatches, it may save your city.)

The Blunt-Billed Rockpecker is small or large, depending upon its sex. No one has been able to determine which is which because both lay eggs in the same nest.

The nest of the Blunt-Billed Rockpecker, like that of the Ruffed Grouse, is built on the ground. But the Rockpecker's nest is from three to six feet in diameter and is carefully constructed to appear exactly like any other piece of woodland earth.

The eggs of the bird look like rocks and come in various sizes and shapes and colors. They are laid either inside or outside of the nest, but nowhere else.

They take a long time to hatch. Some of them hatch, but the rest just lie there.

Hatchlings and chicks have pointed bills. When they leave the nest and begin to search out their own food by pecking at the rocks which may or may not house the Rockworm, the bills of these youngsters, for some reason as yet unknown to naturalists, assume the flat, blunt, beat-up look common to the adult.

The call of the Blunt-Billed Rockpecker is heard only when it is feeding. The careful observer, watching it peck away at a rock, will hear its repeated call: "ah-OOOH-chee, ah-OOOH-chee." The bird is the only member of the woodpecker family that complains of headaches.

Though the preferred and practically exclusive foodstuff of the Blunt-Billed Rockpecker is the Rockworm, the bird will be attracted to feeders on which rocks, aspirin and other such remedies have been scattered.

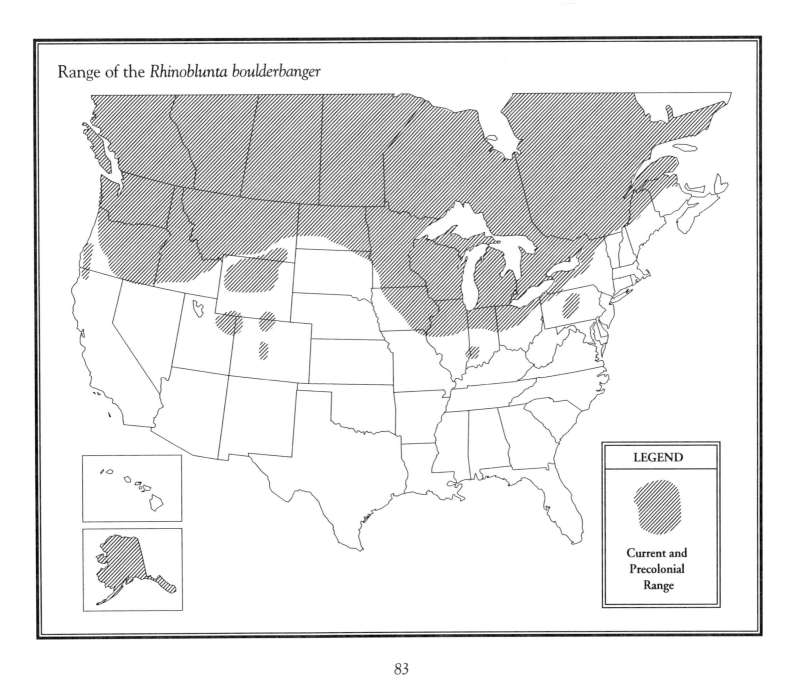

Range of the *Rhinoblunta boulderbanger*

LEGEND

Current and Precolonial Range

AGRO-ARGO-PELTER-POUNDER

(Grantus cashmaximus)

There is a beast that is so uncommon, very few commentators in the entire history of the natural sciences have ever seen it. Much has been said about this fabled northwoods creature. Most of it is wrong.

Various vague and conflicting accounts from lumberjacks and timber cruisers—now long dead—describe the creature. All accounts agree the animal lives in the hollow trunks of large trees. Beyond that point, however, confusion and disagreement are rampant.

For instance, many last-century documents describe it as a hairy, ferocious and savage biped. But some modern scientists believe it is a timid and bashful creature that hides in hollow trees because of its retiring nature—probably because of an unfortunate childhood.

They contend the mysterious creature attacks, then mangles and finally eats human beings only when they come into its extensive territory and can be caught.

Recent interest in this rare creature, and liberal federal funding, have, as of yet, produced no published study or treatise. And this simply because there is no agreement on how the name should be spelled.

The arguments which ensued split the scientific community into three major groups: i.e., those who thought it should be "Agropelter," and those who thought it should be "Argopelter."

Some naturalists claimed the animal pelted its victims with chunks of wood and pine cones. Others contended it pounded the hell out of them with dead tree limbs. This difference of opinion became heated. People lost their tempers and threw things.

The result was to divide naturalists into three

more different camps—one calling themselves the Argo-pounders and the other, the Agro-pounders.

Still other naturalists were tired of the fist fights, the disgraceful cursing and the copious spilling of blood which occured during the scientific discussions of the matter at their Society's annual meetings.

One group attempted to find a middle ground upon which all could agree. It suggested a compromise. The beast could be called the Agro-argo-pelter-pounder. They garnered some support from each of the other groups but met with only limited success.

Unfortunately, the hard-core Agro-pelterists, as well as the Argo-pelterists, the Argo-pounderites and the Agro-pounderites refused to join the Agro-argo-pelter-poundarians.

Moreover, they accused the new group, as well as each other, of being blundering, butterfingered quacks who should stay out of the northwoods legendary animal business and get their governmental grants for studying goats and cows and chickens—the areas of their major experience.

So, now there are five different, mutually antagonistic groups, each contending it is the only true and proper receptacle for the government money which will fund the necessarily lengthy and expensive studies of the habits of the mysterious creature.

Each of the contending groups has a membership of seven scientists. Since they are all married, this means seventy votes can be cast by the entire group in any congressional election. If a politician supports any one of the five groups, he will win fourteen votes—but he will lose fifty-six .

No politician wants to antagonize fifty-six voters by supporting only fourteen others in their pursuit of a government grant of funds for academic studies.

Since no congressional representative will consider an action that might cost him a single vote, the money authorized by a generous Congress for the study of the mysterious beast is lying in the bottom drawer of some bureaucrat's desk in the Department of Health, Education and Profligacy.

But a new development has been reported. It is hinted Professor Norbert Hefflefinger is rounding up a team of fifty married scientists. His group will have one hundred votes. It is expected he will be able to convince his congressional representative that he and his associates are the most qualified applicants for the grant.

The cash will be forthcoming and science will be served.

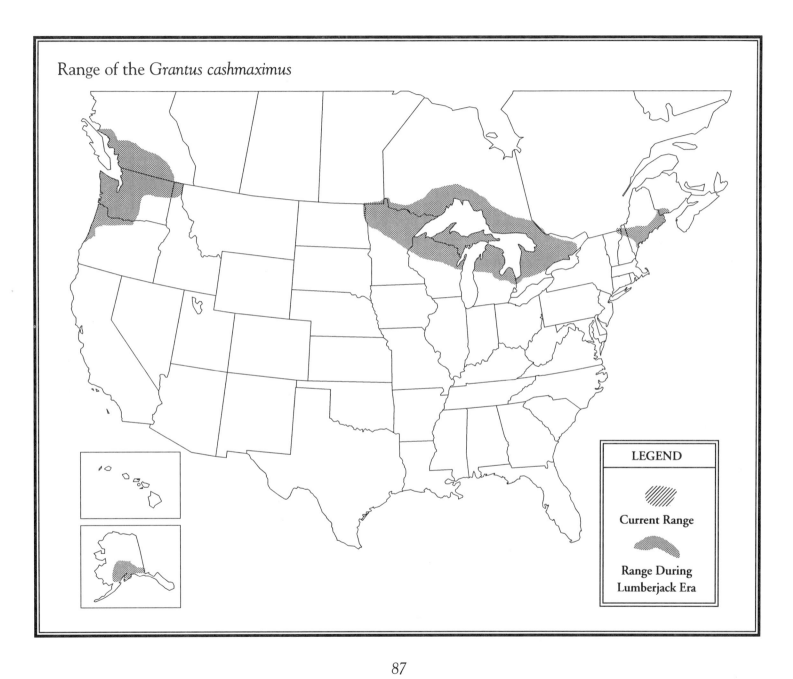

Range of the *Grantus cashmaximus*

LEGEND

Current Range

Range During
Lumberjack Era

THE UPLAND TROUT

(Salmo elevatum)

The beginning of the life cycle of the Upland Trout is unremarkable. The fertilized egg hatches from the gravelly bottom of the cold water stream, and the fry is indistinguishable from other little boy or girl fishies.

But when the larvae of the Brachycentridae family of the order of Trichoptera emerge from their cases, enter the pupa stage and swim to the surface to metamorphose into the adult caddis, then the Upland Trout fry diverge from common troutish patterns and begin their peculiar transformations.

Students of the creature believe the strange life cycle of this species begins when a few young trout dart upwards to feed on the emerging caddis nymphs. Some of them break through the surface of the water and become airborne.

Once in the air, the fry find their situation to be not only exhilarating but also much drier than their previous underwater condition.

Flapping their pectoral and ventral fins, in imitation of the adult caddis, the fish immediately learned to soar through the air. When it has attained full size, the Upland Trout is an accomplished flier and ready for the annual flight to the Yucatan Peninsula.

No Upland Trout have ever been seen returning from their southern migration. As a matter of fact, no one has ever seen one migrating. But they have to go somewhere, don't they? Yucatan naturalists claim they've never seen an Upland Trout. Nobody believes them.

The Upland Trout attains full maturity in three years, at which time the tail and head turn white. Although they are frequently mistaken for eagles, many reports of these magnificent fish soaring through the air have been made.

Upland Trout mate only while flying very high in

the sky. To date, the efforts of the U.S. Fish and Wildlife Service, employing sky divers in an experiment to artificially inseminate the creature, have been unproductive.

Now considered to be one of the few natural enemies of all fish hawks, Upland Trout have been known to chase Ospreys from their territory. The fish commonly takes over the birds' abandoned nests for their own home sites. There they can be seen, surveying their domain and preening their scales.

During the fly hatch, the Upland Trout cruises the streams, flying a foot or so over the water's surface and feeding on mayfly and caddis. Occasionally in its enthusiasm, it will go after an emerging nymph and actually leave the air and become totally immersed in the water.

Since the mature Upland Trout has forgotten how to swim, many drown while engaged in such feedings.

During the 1950's, the Upland Trout population had been reduced to a few breeding pair located in northern Oregon. It was saved from extinction by state game wardens.

If fishermen were found with one in their possession during the May to September trout season, they were promptly arrested and charged with capturing Upland Game without the small game hunting license (which is valid only after the trout season closes).

If a fisherman armed with such a license and a .20 gauge shotgun returned to the Upland Trout country during the October—November bird season and shot one from its lofty perch, he was promptly arrested for fishing out of season.

Rather than run the risk of an olympic-sized fine and the loss of hunting (or fishing) privileges for an extended period, outdoorsmen avoid the Upland Trout as they would avoid the Black Plague. No hunter or fisher will admit to seeing one.

Nevertheless, the fish is commonly found throughout the northwoods. The departments of natural resources of many states have removed the Upland Trout from their endangered species lists. It is now usually placed under the classification entitled "Ridiculous."

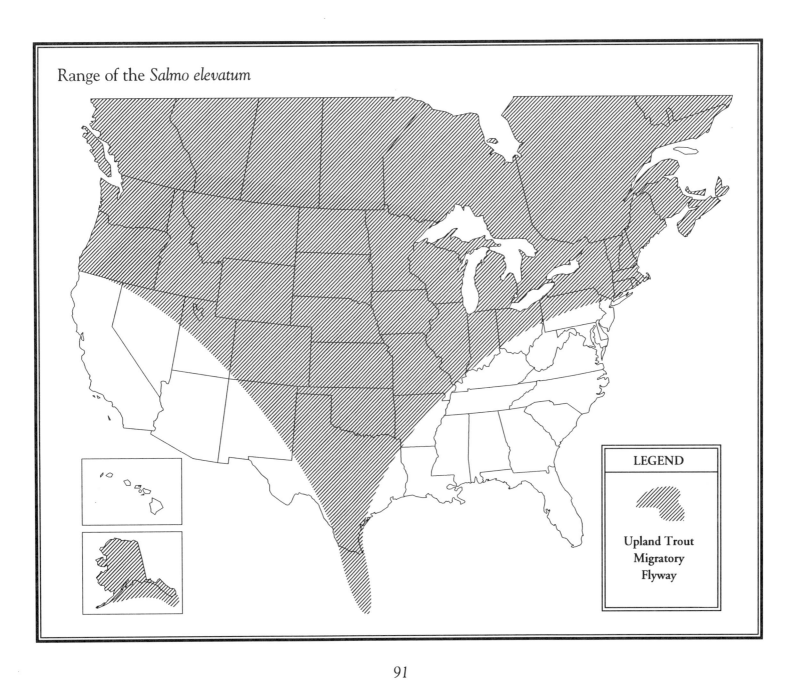

Range of the *Salmo elevatum*

LEGEND

Upland Trout
Migratory
Flyway

91

THE NORTHERN CHIGOE

(Chigo octopodia)

The Chigoe, or as it is commonly called, the chigger, is a small parasitic flea native to tropical portions of the western hemisphere and the southern United States. A member of the Insecta class of the phylum Arthropod, it is a nasty little animal. Ask any dog or cat and it'll tell you.

As the Chigoe migrated to the north, it became larger and larger until, when it reached the Great Lakes, it could no longer subsist on its usual hosts, the ground squirrel, the rat, or the rabbit. It attached itself to more massive mammals.

It attained a size of an inch in diameter and commonly attacked horses and cows. One such specimen attached itself to the hind foot of a cow owned by Mrs. O'Leary. In attempting to kick it off, the cow missed and hit a kerosene lantern by mistake.

And so began the infamous Chigoe fire, which illiterate and bungling journalists misreported as the "Chicago" fire. The fleas were thus responsible for naming one of the largest cities in the country.

In the 1880s, horses purchased in "Chicago" were transported into the northern woods for use in lumber camps. They brought the Chigoe with them.

The frigid temperatures of the pine forests caused the Chigoe to undergo radical changes in its form and life-style. To protect itself from the cold, the insect grew fur and developed into the subspecies known as the Northern Chigoe.

Humane lumbermen, wanting to protect horses from the harassments of the large flea, began to dip their animals in insecticide baths. The practice was

The Northern Chigoe appears at right, under the tail feathers of the mythical gillygalloo, a silly bird known for its square eggs.

effective and the Northern Chigoe had to find another home.

Many fleas sought a new host in the form of the flightless Woodtick Hawk. Though the bird was big and fat enough to provide proper nourishment for the enormous fleas, it did not turn out to be a successful host. The woodticks with which the hawk associated soon attacked the fleas. Whole colonies of them burrowed into the fleas' fur and made life miserable for them. It was sad to see the poor fleas scratching themselves with all eight legs in an attempt to get rid of the pesky ticks.

The extinction of the Woodtick Hawk rang the death knell for those of the Northern Chigoe that had elected the bird as their host.

Others were, temporarily, more successful. They selected the Bobcat. The fleas now had an average length of five inches and their legendary ability to jump had increased proportionately.

A symbiotic relationship between the two species soon developed. As the cat engaged in its wild chase of the rabbit, the fleas hung on its fur for dear life and experienced an exhilaration similar to that felt while on a roller coaster. They loved it. Soon they too joined in the hunt.

When the rabbit, to avoid its pursuer, would execute a full tilt ninety-degree turn, the fleas—using all eight powerful leaping legs—would jump from the side of the Bobcat onto the rabbit, grab its ears and bull dog it to the ground. The cat got the meal and the fleas got one helluva ride.

But all good things must come to an end. At the turn of the century, fashion designers discovered the Northern Chigoe. Its soft and delicate fur was used to line ladies nightgowns. Demand for its pelts skyrocketed. Trappers throughout the north set their clever snares behind the Bobcat's ears. Millions were made at the commodity exchanges. By the end of the First World War, the Northern Chigoe had been trapped into extinction and was no more.

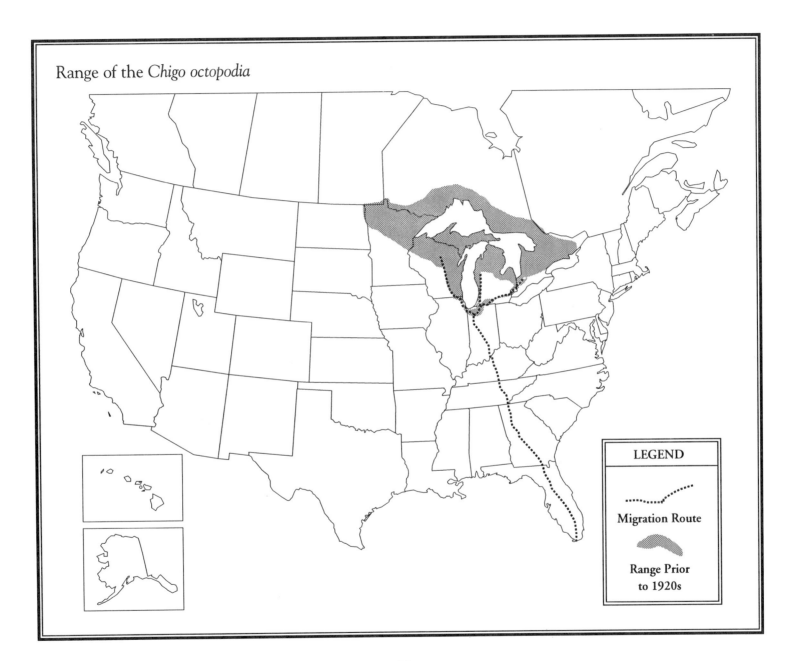

Range of the *Chigo octopodia*

LEGEND

······ Migration Route

▒▒▒ Range Prior
to 1920s

THE SPLINTER CAT

(Quillus transmorgifa)

Mother Nature provides many of her creatures with the ability to evolve when faced with changing environmental factors that affect their ability to survive.

Climatic modifications, variations in food supply and the increase in the number of attacking enemies are all examples of conditions which require an animal to adapt or reserve a place on the extinction list.

The transformations usually occur slowly. Professor Hefflefinger estimates some of them take a hundred years or even more. But occasionally, in crisis situations, the evolutionary process is rapid. The Splinter Cat is a case in point.

The porcupine was created by a committee. Its existence was, quite obviously, allowed without appropriate oversight. Almost immediately questions were asked: Have our design people made a terrible mistake? Will this animal be able to reproduce?

Rather than wait for answers (and under the assumption the animal would soon become extinct), the Splinter Cat was created. The basic concept of the porcupine was retained, but its original quill pattern was modified. In the Splinter Cat model they point forwards instead of backwards.

However, the porcupine fooled everybody and found a way to reproduce. Now there were two species that fit the exact same ecological niche. Environmental activists were thus faced with a serious problem.

With two animals eating the inner bark of the popple, the tree could become extinct, and that was a no-no. The alternative of killing off one of the species was equally unattractive.

While the debate raged within the activist groups, the Splinter Cats solved the problem without help from anyone. After carefully considering the

matter, they decided the inner bark of trees didn't taste very good anyway. They elected to change their eating habits.

From that day forward, the Splinter Cats fed only on those foods which contained a high glucose content. The decision required further adaptations and soon two subspecies of Splinter Cat evolved.

The Maple Splinter Cat developed a single, hollow, protruding horn-like mouth. This subspecies feeds in the early springtime. It bores into the Sugar Maple when the sap begins to run. It fasts for the rest of the year, but occasionally competes with bumble bees and other insects for the nectar produced by wild flowers.

The other subspecies, the Honey Splinter Cat, redesigned its own face. It became a very tough, heavy and squarish box-like protuberance. The mouth and nose migrated to the bottom side of the box. The snout became a hard, flat surface. The face of the Honey Splinter Cat is now reminiscent of a twenty-pound maul.

The Honey Splinter Cat is a fall feeder. It fasts in the winter, spring and summer. During those seasons it wanders through the woods in search of trees containing colonies of honey bees.

In the autumn, when the honey has been produced, the Honey Splinter Cat repeatedly charges the tree and pounds it with his hammerhead until it crashes to the ground. Then it smashes the trunk open and devours the honey at its leisure.

A shy and retiring animal, the Honey Splinter Cat eschews human company and is seldom if ever seen by woodsmen. The number of fallen trees found throughout the northern forests testify to its presence.

Naturalists applaud the transmogrifications of the beast. To distinguish it from the porcupine, they no longer need to get close to one and study the direction in which its quills are growing. They now need only look at the shape of the creature's head.

Those who insist upon following the old time identification procedures frequently obtain first-hand experience on how to remove quills from one's person.

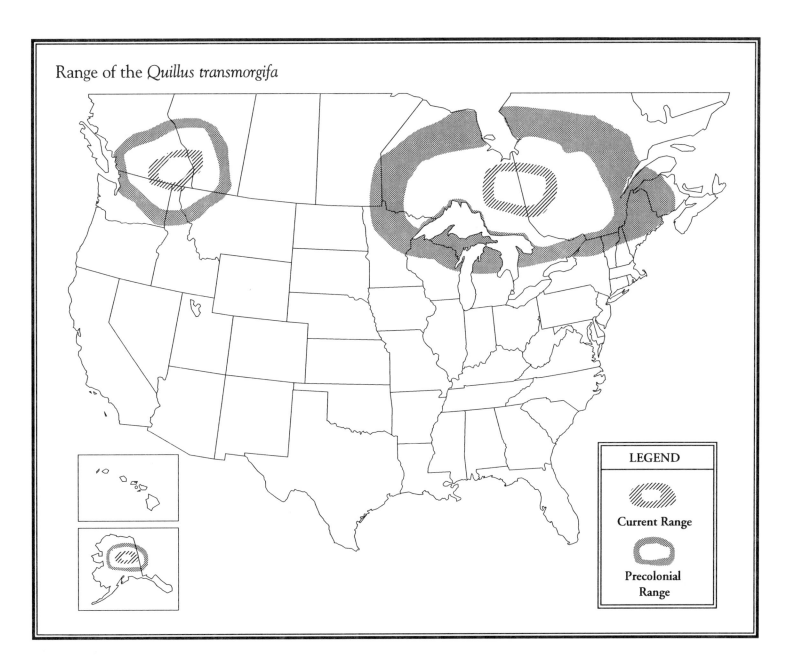

Range of the *Quillus transmorgifa*

LEGEND

Current Range

Precolonial Range

THE SHOVEL-NOSED BEAVER

(Castor unfamiliaria)

One hundred and fifty years ago, the common beaver (*Castor canadensis*) and its various subspecies were found throughout what is now the United States, excepting, of course, Hawaii. The animals apparently felt it was a nice place to visit, but they didn't want to live there.

Certainly the number of beaver in North American streams approached the astronomical. Professor Norbert Hefflefinger assigns two reasons for the abundance of the creature.

First, the Native Americans did not wear stove pipe hats, and, second, to the delight of the some-times constipated Indian kids, they had not yet invented castor oil. During the first half of the 19th century, the men's hat industry would use nothing but beaver pelt to make the fine felt found in quality hats. The beaver was in demand.

Both the Hudson Bay Company and John Jacob Astor's America Fur Company were organized primarily for the trapping and collection of beaver pelts. The creature was trapped nearly to extinction.

One rare subspecies was able to avoid the depre-dations of the trapper. The Shovel-Nosed Beaver attracted no interest from the fur companies because it had no fur whatsoever.

Some claim the Shovel-Nosed Beaver migrated north from south of the border, where it enjoyed an ancestry common with that of the Mexican Hairless Chihuahua. Others really couldn't care less. They are only interested in the fact that the range of the Shovel-Nose was limited to Upper Michigan, north-ern Wisconsin, Minnesota and the provinces of Manitoba and Ontario—some of the coldest parts of the country.

The uninitiated might think that the hairless condition of the Shovel-Nosed Beaver did not lend

it to life in the northwoods. And they would be right. All members of the family should have frozen to death.

To explain its survival, a review of the characteristics of the two animals is in order. The common beaver cuts down trees and floats them around in streams until they are placed in the proper position for dam building. It cuts branches of aspen, cottonwood, alder, willow and birch, which it places under water near its lodge for its winter supply of food.

The flat tail of the common beaver is used as a rudder and propeller, as an alarm signal (when slapped against the water), and as a trowel for applying mud to dams. The tail is also used to sit upon as it squats near the tree it is about to chew down.

The Shovel-Nose can't chew trees or branches. Its big nose gets in the way. But it is a much more efficient dam builder. With a nose that looks and can operate just like its flat tail, the Shovel-Nose can swim forwards and then backwards without turning around. That saves time.

It can give a double alarm, slapping both nose and tail against the water at the same time. Using its nose as the trowel, the Shovel-Nose can see exactly what it is doing. It makes very neat dams.

The common beaver works with his tail, can't see what he is doing and usually ends up with messy mud work. The Shovel-Nose Beaver negotiated symbiotic contracts with the common beaver that allowed it to survive. While the common beaver was busy cutting and storing branches for its winter food supply, the Shovel-Nose was building and repairing the lodges and dams. In exchange for the construction work, the Shovel-Nose was allowed to stay in the common beaver's lodge and snuggle in with the colony, keeping cozy, warm and well fed throughout the winter.

And with a nose that looked exactly like a beaver's tail, it could stand on its head. Thus, the Shovel-Nose also provided entertainment when the rest of the colony suffered from cabin fever.

The Shovel-Nosed Beaver was never found in abundance. With a front end which looked exactly like its back end, successful mating was rare.

But it was the lumberjack who caused the extinction of the animal. A popular form of their entertainment, second only to log rolling, was log racing. Lumberjacks would straddle logs and race down river. Since paddles and oars were difficult to come by in the woods, the Shovel-Nosed Beavers were captured, killed, and mummified. The lumberjacks would then use them like kayak paddles. Soon the subspecies was no more.

Range of the *Castor unfamiliaria*

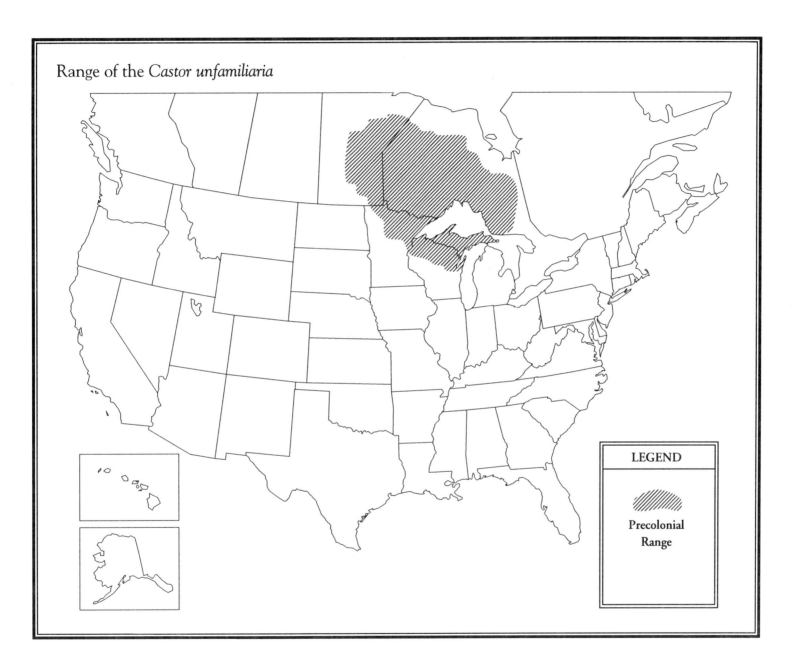

LEGEND

Precolonial
Range

THE RINGERSNAKE

(Crotalus giganticus [venomous])

The most popular poisonous snakes in North America are the coral snake and the rattlesnake, neither of which are found in the northwoods. The following information is given as a public service to those of you who insist upon living in or traveling to other parts of the country.

The coral snake is very dangerous and can be identified by its bright red, yellow and black rings. The nonvenomous corn snake and others wear the same colors, but their pattern and arrangement are different.

In distinguishing between the poisonous and nonpoisonous red, black and yellow snakes, the following Native American aphorism is helpful: "If the red touches the yellow, run away. If the red does not touch the yellow, run away."

The diamondback rattlesnake is a pit viper. It can grow to be five to six feet long and is identified by the diamond scale pattern on its back and by the series of horny cylindrical rings found at the tip of its tail.

When the snake is disturbed, it vibrates its tail, the rings knock against each other and a rattling sound is produced. Because of this characteristic, the snake gets the name of diamondback.

Professor Norbert Hefflefinger believes the rattlesnake evolved from the Woodland Ringersnake. The Ringersnake can be recognized by its solid, heavy tail and the flat, equally hard plate located on the top of its head.

When the Ringersnake is disturbed, it bangs its tail against its head and sends out a ringing sound much like that made by the camp cook's iron triangle when used to call the men to dinner.

The young of the Ringersnake are born with their peculiar flat, hard head. About three feet long, they

have the same size, color and shape of a double-bitted axe.

Many a lumberjack has been surprised to spit on his hands, pick up his axe, swing it back preparatory to chopping down a tree, only to find the handle so pliable it would wind itself around his neck and give him a heavy blow to the forehead.

Often the curious reptile was brought back to camp where it would be slipped into the bunk of a tenderfoot or given to a comrade to sharpen.

Camp cooks tamed the reptile and taught it to ring on command. They could then busy themselves with cookhouse chores and send the snake outside to sound the call that would bring the men in from the woods.

The immature Ringersnake's bite is not toxic, although its diet consists solely of poison ivy, poison oak, deadly nightshade and the death-cap Amanita mushroom. It is believed the ingested poisons accumulate, and when the reptile has attained a length of only twenty feet, its bite becomes extremely venomous.

During the lumber camp days, the domesticated Ringersnake was killed as soon as it grew nineteen and one half feet long and was still in its developmental stage. The snake was then skinned and its hide stretched over the iron bands on the wooden wheels of the loggers' wagons.

The snake's skin protected the iron from damage caused by running over rocks in the summer, and, in the winter, its nubbly surface served the same purpose as the modern snow tire.

The shedded skins of the Ringer were much valued by the lumberjacks, who made boots from the thick waterproof hide.

As it matured in the wild, the Ringersnake not only became venomous but also attained its legendary size. In its need for larger and more nutritious foods to fuel its enormous body, the Ringer sought out human prey.

Camp records report an instance where the snake bit into a rock on one side of the river and wrapped its tail around one on the other. Its huge body stretched across the river and caused a log jam. Men were sent to pick their way across the jumble of logs, set dynamite at the key places and blow the jam. While they were working at their tasks, the reptile shot out of the water, grabbed three of them and return to the depths. They were never seen again.

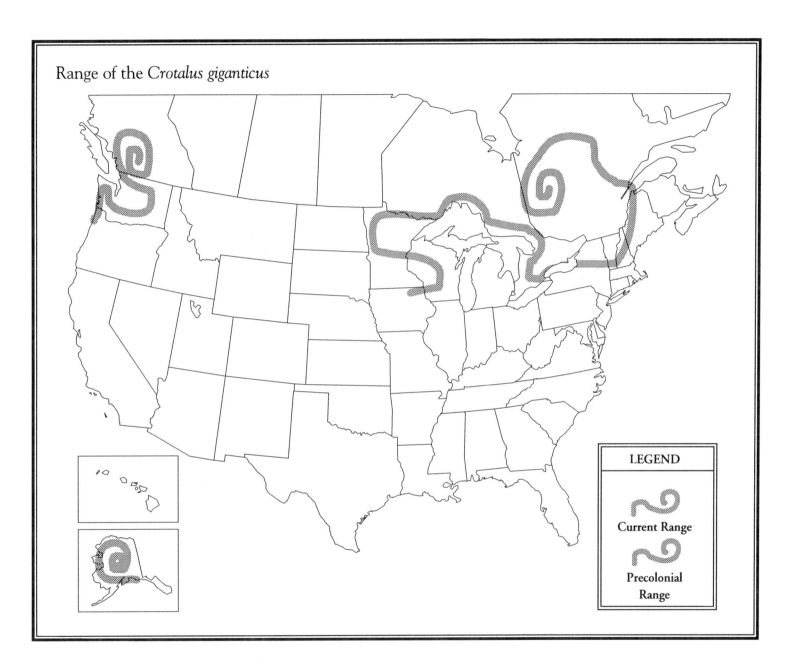

Range of the *Crotalus giganticus*

LEGEND

Current Range

Precolonial Range

THE POLAR PIKE

(Esox giganticus nordica)

Many animals historically found in the northwoods moved there specifically to find more miserable landscapes, colder temperatures and harsher living conditions.

There can be no other logical reason why the Arctic Fox, the Snowy Owl and the Polar Bear live in the frigid and windswept tundra. They must like it up there. They are all mobile, and if they didn't like it, they could move back south where they came from.

Some creatures consider pain, distress and unnecessary agony to be serious annoyances. They don't enjoy them. As a result, some of them move from cities to northern towns. And some who have given the Arctic a fair chance move out and seek a more favorable environment. The Polar Pike is an example.

It was tired of eating Polar Bears and Seal blubber and with being uncomfortable with the inactivity caused by being frozen in a block of ice for six months of the year. It longed for those perfect places advertised on the travel posters. It had enough of the Arctic life-style. The Polar Pike decided to search for a new home. Its wanderings were extensive. The fish lived a nomadic existence and established no permanent residence for years.

The first migration was to the Caribbean. The lure of the sun, the sand and the tropical breezes had called. They swam down to Jamaica. But all did not go well. Although the fish developed a taste for Sea Turtles and Sand Sharks, they could not become accustomed to the salty water. And, as tourists, they were charged the highest prices. It wasn't easy earning the money to pay for both room and meals. All the Polar Pike abandoned Jamaica in a body. The population split into two schools. One went north and the other headed for the Rockies. The school that traveled west had a difficult journey, flopping

through the deserts of Texas and New Mexico, but they eventually arrived in Colorado.

They wiggled up the mountains where they enjoyed the cooler weather and abundant food. After depleting the mountain goat population, they started eating elk. It was a terrible error. The elk horns got stuck in their throats and made further feeding impossible. And so the Colorado branch of the Polar Pike species became extinct. (The state recognized their tragedy by naming a peak after them.)

The school that traveled north had an easier time. Swimming through the Everglades, they were bothered by the Florida mosquitoes and chigoes. But the abundance of alligators provided them with more than ample food. All went well until they jumped and squirmed through Pikeville (the seat of Pike County in Eastern Kentucky).

There they took the wrong turn and ended up near Philadelphia. When the error was discovered, they immediately did an about-face and flopped away as fast as possible. Later, in commemoration of the event, the route they took to escape from the state was named the Pennsylvania Turnpike.

Once in Lake Erie, the Polar Pike found migration much easier and soon reached Lake Superior. Individuals spread up the rivers into their present homes, the woodland lakes of the north country from Alaska to Maine.

Diminutive members of the Pike family—like the Pickerel, the Northern Pike, and the Muskellunge—soon joined the Polar Pike, and the basis for the area's now famous freshwater sport fishing industry was created.

Once located in the northern freshwater lakes and surrounded by its own kind, the Polar Pike prospered. The temperature extremes were well within their comfort limits, and the presence of the Muskellunge provided them with adequate food.

The smaller Muskies—five feet and under—are able to swim through the gills of the Polar Pike and survive to provide an adequate breeding stock for its species. Larger Muskies are rare because they are usually eaten by the big Pike.

Some companies make muskie lures. The plugs are four feet long and look a good deal like a Muskellunge. They probably would fool a Polar Pike, and he might strike one. However, they are very difficult to cast, especially when attached to the woven cable fishing line recommended for Polar Pike fishing. The Polar Pike, as a result, has never been caught with rod and reel.

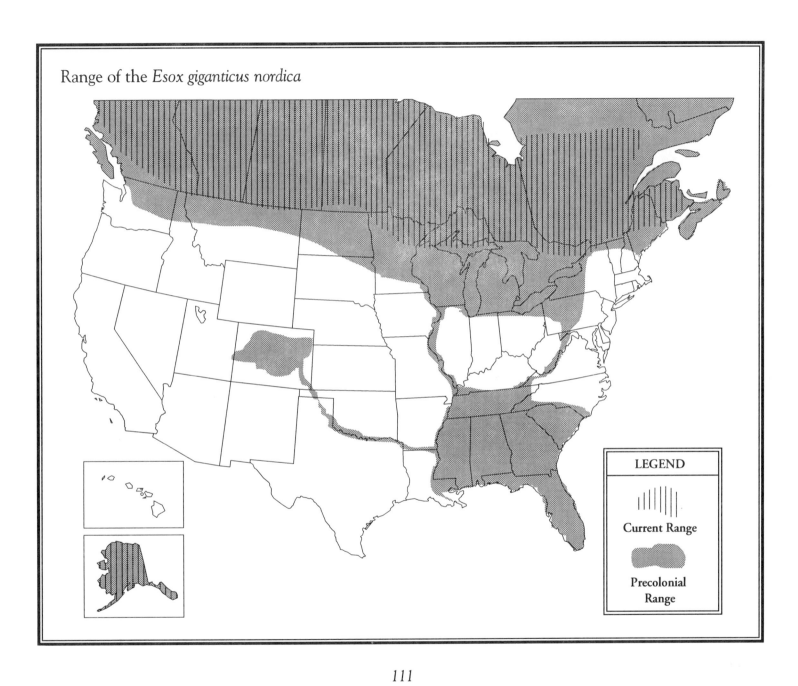

Range of the *Esox giganticus nordica*

LEGEND

Current Range

Precolonial Range

THE TWEE BIRD

(Contractus fulfillamum)

(Publisher's Note: The Author contracted to write a book containing 18,000 words. Until he sent this, his last story, he was only 131 words short.)

The Twee Bird is a small multicolored bird that comes to the aid of people in distress. Its plaintive call is:

Twee, Twee.

Part II

Unauthenticated Mythical Animals

NOTE: For this final section of our little tome, we are indebted to Mr. William Cox, author of *Fearsome Creatures of the Lumberwoods*, from which the following descriptions are drawn. Mr. Cox's natural history credentials are impeccable: A graduate of the first forestry class at the University of Minnesota; Minnesota's first State Forester (1911) and first Conservation Commissioner (1931). The editors, having no reason to doubt his veracity, are pleased to present these vivid and scientifically valuable animal profiles.

Author Galen Winter, however, fearing the possibility of splitting royalties with the Cox estate, put up quite a stink. Having already snookered Dr. Norbert Hefflefinger out of any compensation for his enormous contribution to this volume, Mr. Winter insisted that, absent of artist John Boettcher's scratchboard engravings, the following creatures could not be visually verified or authenticated.

As is customary in the book publishing field, author and editor negotiated and a compromise was struck: We told him we would delete this section, and then, for the selfless sake of science, included it anyway.

THE HUGAG

(Rythmopes inarticulatus)

The hugag is a huge animal of the Lake States. Its range includes western Wisconsin, northern Minnesota, and a territory extending indefinitely northward in the Canadian wilds toward Hudson Bay.

In size the hugag may be compared to the moose, and in form it somewhat resembles that animal. Very noticeable, however, are its jointless legs, which compel the animal to remain on its feet, and its long upper lip, which prevents it from grazing. If it tried that method of feeding it would simply tramp its upper lip into the dirt. Its head and neck are leathery and hairless; its strangely corrugated ears flop downward; its four-toed feet, long bushy tail, shaggy coat and general make-up give the beast an unmistakably prehistoric appearance. The hugag has a perfect mania for traveling, and few hunters who have taken up its trail ever came up with the beast or back to camp. It is reported to keep going all day long, browsing on twigs, flopping its lip around trees, and stripping bark as occasion offers, and at night, since it cannot lie down, it leans against a tree, bracing its hind legs and marking time with its front ones. The most successful hugag hunters have adopted the practice of notching trees so that they are almost ready to fall, and when the hugag leans up against one, both the tree and the animal come down. In its helpless condition it is then easily dispatched. The last one killed, so far as known, was on Turtle River in northern Minnesota, where a young one weighing 1,800 pounds was found stuck in the mud.

THE GUMBEROO

(Megalogaster repercussus)

In the foggy region along the Pacific Coast from Grays Harbor to Humboldt Bay there ranges a kind of creature that has caused much annoyance in the lumber woods. This is the gumberoo, which luckily is so rare that only once in a great while is one seen. It is believed to remain in hiding most of the time in the base of enormous, burned-out cedar trees, from where it sallies forth occasionally on frightful marauding expeditions. During these periods of activity the beast is always hungry and devours anything it can find that looks like food. A whole horse may be eaten at one sitting, distending the gumberoo out of all proportions, but failing to appease its hunger or cause it the slightest discomfort.

The specimens seen are reported to have been coal black, but that may have been due to their being smirched with the charred wood. In size the beast corresponds closely to a black bear, for which it might be mistaken only for the fact that the gumberoo is almost hairless. To be sure, it has prominent eyebrows and some long, bristly hairs on its chin, but the body is smooth, tough, and shiny and bears not even a wrinkle. The animal is a tireless traveler when looking for food, but is not swift in its movements or annoyed in the slightest degree by the presence of enemies. The latter characteristic is easily accounted for by the fact that no other animal within its range has ever found a successful method of attacking a gumberoo or a vulnerable spot in one's anatomy. Whatever strikes the beast bounces off with the same force. Its elastic hide hurls back with equal ease the charging elk and the wrathy hornet. A rock or peavey thrown at the creature bounds back at whoever threw it.

It is believed that the scarcity of gumberoos is due to their combustible character and the prevalence of forest fires. The animal burns, like celluloid, with explosive force. Frequently during and after a forest fire in the heavy cedar near Coos Bay, woodmen have insisted that they heard loud reports quite unlike the sound of falling trees, and detected the smell of burning rubber in the air.

THE BILLDAD

(Saltipiscator falcorostratus)

If you have ever paddled around Boundary Pond in northwest Maine at night, you have probably heard from out the black depths of a cove a spat like a paddle striking the water. It may have been a paddle, but the chances are ten to one that it was a billdad fishing. This animal occurs only on this one pond, in Hurricane Township. It is about the size of a beaver, but has long, kangaroo-like hind legs, short front legs, webbed feet, and a heavy, hawk-like bill. Its mode of fishing is to crouch on a grassy point overlooking the water, and when a trout rises for a bug, to leap with amazing swiftness just past the fish, bringing its heavy, flat tail down with a resounding smack over him. This stuns the fish, which is immediately picked up and eaten by the billdad. It has been reported that sixty yards is an average jump for an adult male. Up to three years ago the opinion was current among lumber jacks that the billdad was fine eating, but since the beasts are exceedingly shy and hard to catch no one was able to remember having tasted the meat. That fall one was killed on Boundary Pond and brought into the Great Northern Paper Company's camp on Hurricane Lake, where the cook made a most savory slumgullion of it. The first and only man to taste it was Bill Murphy, a tote-road swamper from Ambegegis. After the first mouthful his body stiffened, his eyes glazed, and his hands clutched the table edge. With a wild yell he rushed out of the cook-house, down to the lake, and leaped clear out fifty yards, coming down in a sitting posture—exactly like a billdad catching a fish. Of course, he sank like a stone. Since then not a lumber jack in Maine will touch billdad meat, not even with a pike pole.

THE SNOW WASSET

(Mustelinopsis subitivorax)

On the most northern logging camps of Canada we hear of the snow wasset. This is surely an animal of the Boreal Zone. It is a migratory animal, wintering in the lumbering region between the Great Lakes and Hudson Bay and spending its summers far north in Labrador and the Barren Grounds. Unlike most wild creatures of the North, the wasset is said to hibernate during only the warmest weather, when its hair turns green and it curls up in a cranberry marsh. During the summer it has rudimentary legs, which enable it to creep slowly around and remain in the shade.

After the first howling snowstorm the wasset sheds its legs and starts south, dipping about in the snow. It soon attains remarkable skill in this method of travel, which enables it to surprise burrowing grouse, crouching rabbits, and skulking varmints of many kinds. Later in the winter, when food becomes scarce and more difficult to obtain, even wolves are seized from below and dragged howling and kicking into the snowdrifts. According to woodmen, the tragedies of the far North are more numerous beneath the crusted snow than above it. There is no telling how many creatures are pulled down and eaten by the wasset, for this animal has a voracious appetite, comparable only to that of the wolverine, but since it is four times as big and forty times as active as the wolverine it must eat correspondingly more.

The only specimen of this beast ever examined by white men was an imperfect one on James Bay, where a party of surveyors found an Indian in a peculiar canoe which upon examination was shown to be made from one wasset hide greatly stretched. There being no leg holes in the white winter pelt, it is peculiarly adapted to the making of shapely one-man canoes, which are said to be used also as sleds by the Indians. A whole battery of dead-falls are believed to be used in trapping a wasset, since it is impossible to tell in what direction the animal's body may extend. The trigger is set so that a dozen logs fall in from all sides toward the bait, pinning the animal under the snow wherever he may be.

THE WAPALOOSIE

(Geometrigradus cilioretractus)

In the damp forests of the Pacific coast and eastward as far as the St. Joe River in north Idaho ranges a quaint little beast, known among loggers as the wapaloosie. It is about the size of a sausage dog, but is not even distantly related to the canine family. The wapaloosie, according to lumberjacks, lives upon shelf fungus exclusively, and he is able to get them with ease, no matter if they are growing on the tip-top of a hundred-foot dead tree. It is a pleasure for one of these animals to climb, for he has feet and toes like those of a woodpecker, and he humps himself along like a measuring worm. Even his tail is spiked at the tip and aids him as he mounts the lofty firs in quest of food. One of the most peculiar features of the animal was discovered only recently. A lumberjack in one of the camps on the Humptulips River in Washington shot a wapaloosie, and upon examining its velvety coat decided that it would make an attractive and serviceable pair of mittens, which he proceeded to make. The hide was tanned thoroughly and the mittens made with care, fur side out, and as the lumber jack went to work he exhibited them with pride. Imagine his surprise upon taking hold of an ax to find that the mittens immediately worked their way up and off the handle. It was the same with whatever he took hold of, and finding that he could not use the mittens, they were left in a skid road, and were last seen working their way over logs and litter across the slashing.

THE TOTE-ROAD SHAGAMAW

(Bipedester delusissimus)

From the Rangeley Lakes to the Allegash and across in New Brunswick loggers tell of an animal which has puzzled many a man, even those who were not strangers in the woods. Frequently the report is circulated that the tracks of a bear have been seen near camp, but a little later this is denied and moose tracks are reported instead. Heated argument among the men, sometimes resulting in fist fights, are likely to follow. It is rightly considered an insult to a woodsman to accuse him of not being able to distinguish the track of either of these animals. To only a few of the old timber cruisers and river men is the explanation of these changing tracks known.

Gus Demo, of Oldtown, Maine, who has hunted and trapped and logged in the Maine woods for 40 years, once came upon what he recognized as the tracks of a moose. After following it for about 80 rods it changed abruptly into unmistakable bear tracks; another 80 rods and it changed to moose tracks again. It was soon observed by Mr. Demo that these changes took place precisely every quarter of a mile, and, furthermore, that whatever was making the tracks always followed a tote road or a blazed line through the woods. Coming up within sight of the animal, Gus saw that it had front feet like a bear's and hind feet like those of a moose, and that it was pacing carefully, taking exactly a yard at a step. Suddenly it stopped, looked all about, and swung as on a pivot, then inverting itself and, walking on its front feet only, it resumed its pacing. Mr. Demo was only an instant in recognizing by the witness trees that the place where the animal changed was a section corner. From this fact he reasoned that the shagamaw must have been originally a very imitative animal which, from watching surveyors, timber cruisers, and trappers patiently following lines through the woods, contracted the habit itself. He figures that the shagamaw can count only as high as 40; therefore it must invert itself every quarter of a mile.